Springer Books on Professional Computing

Edited by Henry Ledgard

Bruce D. Sanders

Computer Confidence

A Human Approach to Computers

With 23 Figures

Springer-Verlag
New York Berlin Heidelberg Tokyo

Bruce D. Sanders
700 Brookside Drive
Vacaville, California 95688
U.S.A.

Series Editor
Henry Ledgard
Human Factors Ltd.
Leverett, Massachusetts 01054
U.S.A.

Library of Congress Cataloging in Publication Data
Sanders, Bruce D.
   Computer confidence.
   (Springer books on professional computing)
   Includes index.
   1. Electronic data processing—Management.
2. Electronic data processing—Psychological aspects.
I. Title. II. Title.
QA76.9.M3S26 1983   658.4′0388   83-16996

Typeset by Ampersand Inc., Rutland, Vermont.
Printed and bound by R. R. Donnelley & Sons, Harrisonburg, Virginia.
Printed in the United States of America.

9 8 7 6 5 4 3 2 1

ISBN 0-387-90917-6 Springer-Verlag New York Berlin Heidelberg Tokyo
ISBN 3-540-90917-6 Springer-Verlag Berlin Heidelberg New York Tokyo

Preface

Much of the material in this book comes from what I've learned as I've traveled around the country conducting seminars about working profitably in the automated office. During the first few months of those seminars, there was a question I was asked more often than any other single question. I was asked the question so often that I gave it a nickname. I called it my "What The Devil" question. Often in different words, usually at the morning break in the seminar, and almost always with an effort not to offend or embarrass, I was asked, "What the devil is a psychologist doing conducting seminars about computer systems?"

I'm not asked "What the Devil" questions much anymore. Those familiar with office automation have come to realize that human factors chiefly determine whether a computer system will be a success or an expensive failure. So many computer systems have not gained acceptance by employees because the planners didn't use good psychological sense. That is especially true as the computers move from the Engineering Department into the executive suites and the role of computers changes from just producing paper into also assisting in managerial decision making.

One human factor I've learned is that people would much rather skip around in a book than read it from front cover to back cover directly. It's true whether the book is a user manual for office equipment or a volume on computer systems for decision makers. Chances are you've already browsed through this book, and I encourage you to continue doing so. For one thing, you're more likely to see how the various themes fit together.

I've tried to place material where it has proven to be of interest to the manager who is not a data processing professional. This has resulted in some ideas being introduced in places that might seem unusual to a computer engineer. For instance, batch processing is defined in the chapter on video display terminals and the notion of parallel operation appears in the chapter on end-user surveys. The brief index is designed to help you locate definitions that might be out of logical order for you as well as locate all material relating to the major ideas of the text.

The mechanics of preparing this manuscript were much easier because of the superb secretarial help of Lynne Wallace, the abilities of artist Brian Tefft, the talents of various computerized devices, and the patience and understanding of my family. I am grateful to them all.

Contents

Chapter 9

Chapter 10

Index

Computer Confidence

A Human Approach to Computers

Chapter 1

Fiche & Chip Decision Making

When computers first came in the door of business, nonprofit, and government organizations, they were assigned the boring tasks. Computers, and the people who ran the computers, made out paychecks. They kept inventory records. They kept a tally of who owed how much to whom. But now computers are doing fancier work. They are helping employees make sophisticated decisions. "What would probably happen to sales if we cut prices by 15 percent? Would profits go up in the first year? How about in successive years?" "If our budget is cut 15 percent, what are the best ways to spend the available funds? What are our best arguments for getting that 15 percent restored?"

It isn't that computers are making all these decisions on their own—at least not yet. It is, instead, a matter of computer systems providing to people the right information at the right time in the right form so that those people can make the best decisions. Computers have been promoted from payroll clerks to administrative assistants.

This means that computer systems have to be designed to get along well with people. When a limited number of staff had full responsibility for interacting with the computers, those staff could be selected for their ability to adjust to machine languages and machine procedures. But if there is to be a computer terminal on the desk of almost every employee and if those employees are going to use the terminals, then obscure languages and complex procedures are completely unacceptable.

Computer systems that earn their promotions from payroll clerks to administrative assistants do so by being *user friendly*. A system that people can easily learn to use, that provides them answers quickly and reliably, and

Figure 1.1   Three computer system functions.

that adjusts to their differing styles of making decisions is a user-friendly computer system.

Other definitions of user friendliness come from the way you conceptualize the computer system. One view is in terms of function. There are three basic functions in a computer system: input, processing, and output. As seen in Figure 1.1, raw data come into the system. They are processed in ways that make the data more valuable, and the result of this processing is the output of the system.

The data may be more valuable because they are reclassified in some way. For example, suppose your organization sells many different items in many different sales locations. It would be valuable to know how well each of the items is selling. The computer system could have as input the record of each sales transaction and could produce as output overall sales for each type of item for all sales locations.

Value may come from fancy arithmetic calculations. Suppose your organization operates a chain of nursing homes, and you'd like to build a new facility in a promising location. Evaluation of each candidate as a building site would include sophisticated calculations combining information about average age of people in that area, average income of people in that area, and building costs, among other factors. In some cases, the assumptions and calculations would be especially complicated. For instance, the location should not have too many medical facilities, since this would provide excessive competition, but not too few, either, since you want a pool of skilled staff in the area who can be recruited as employees and consultants or used as referral sources.

Value can come from changing numbers to graphs or putting information on paper in the form of electronic signals, which are less expensive to store than paper. Each of these is a type of task computer systems do well, and each can be seen in terms of input, processing, and output.

Going along with this view, *data processing* can be defined as the use of computers to change data into a more valuable form. The change might be a matter of simple arithmetic calculations. Or it might be grouping the data, summarizing it, and calculating trends. It might be searching through the data for exceptions to trends so that these exceptions can be brought to the attention of the users of the system.

In its administrative assistant role, the computer system should provide information as output. *Information* means facts with implications for action. A common error made by non-data-processing staff is purchasing facts without adequate attention to how the facts will help in decision making. They should ask, "Will the output from the system clearly help me make decisions that move my organization towards its goals?" If the answer is no, spend your organization's money on some other decorations for the office because the computer machinery certainly won't earn its keep.

The functional view goes at least a little beyond input–processing–output because the system needs places for storage. Much of the reason for storage has to do with the extremely fast processing speed of the computer. The part of the computer that does the processing is called the CPU or *central processing unit*. It performs the arithmetic operations, like adding, subtracting, multiplying, and dividing. It performs logical operations, like comparing a word you type with a word in the system dictionary to judge if you spelled the word correctly. And the CPU coordinates actions of other parts of the system.

Large CPUs process millions of numbers every second, and even the slowest CPUs process data many times faster than a person can type it in. When there is a storage function in the system, data can be accumulated and then put into the CPU all at once. The type of storage used here is called a *buffer*. A buffer stores information temporarily. On the input side of the system, the buffer might hold a few hundred words or numbers, and then when it is full, it can empty its contents into the CPU at electronic speed. Between the times that the buffer from the input terminal is emptying its contents, the CPU can work on other chores, such as receiving information from buffers of other input terminals. Such systems are called *time sharing*, multiuser, multitasking, or some other name that indicates the CPU is serving a number of input terminals.

On the output side, a buffer also can be useful. The output might appear on a printed page, and even the fastest printer can't produce paper as quickly as the CPU can transfer the information. When the printer has a buffer, the CPU can place the information in that buffer at electronic speed and move on to other tasks. The printer then calls up the information from the buffer in turn.

Figure 1.2 illustrates where buffers fit into the computer system. They are a type of storage, but because they are usually located within input and output devices, they usually are not diagrammed as separate items. In a listing of computer system functions, "input" refers to "input devices including buffers," and "output" refers to "output devices including buffers."

Figure 1.2   Where buffers fit in.

Another type of storage keeps output in a form the computer can later read. By having data on magnetic tapes or magnetic disks, there is quick, handy access to the CPU. A third reason for storage is that it gives the CPU a place to keep intermediate results, as when it is adding numbers, calculating subtotals, and then coming up with a grand total. The subtotals can be stored and then used for obtaining the grand total.

There are two types of storage in the computer system. One, most often called *main memory*, primary memory, or internal memory, is characterized by very fast *access time*. That is, the CPU can get to main memory contents with extreme speed. For reasons of efficiency, every item of data being processed by the CPU and every instruction telling the CPU what to do with the data is placed in main memory.

Secondary memory is the name given to devices like punched paper cards, magnetic tape, diskettes or floppy disks, hard disks, and bubble memories. These are methods for storing data, or information, for a longer period of time than in main memory. Compared to main memory, secondary memory has a much slower access time, but it is less expensive. You can have only so much main memory, limited by the cost and by the number of connections available to the CPU. But once you obtain a device, called a *tape drive*, for reading data from a magnetic tape, you can buy as many tapes as your shelf space and budget allow.

There is another important difference between main memory and secondary memory. Although important exceptions to this exist, main memory is generally *volatile*. This means that when the electrical power goes off and then goes on again, the memory traces have disappeared into the ether of the universe, never to be seen again. However, secondary memory is always *nonvolatile*. Even if the electrical power goes off, the memory traces, in the form of punch holes or magnetic traces, will still be there when the power is turned on again.

Figure 1.3 illustrates the functional view of the computer system. Notice that because everything must enter main memory before being processed by the CPU, the CPU and main memory are considered to be an inseparable unit. Also, notice that information can enter the CPU/main memory unit from storage, not just exit from the CPU/main memory unit to storage. That is, information can be retrieved by the CPU from a magnetic tape or magnetic disk as well as be recorded under direction of the CPU onto a magnetic tape or magnetic disk.

A definition of user friendliness from the functional view concerns mostly input and output. Does the system capture the right kinds of data for input, and is data input quick and accurate? Is information output in a form convenient to use, and does it arrive on the decision maker's desk in time to be most useful? Is the system flexible enough to adjust to changes in data availability or requirements for data input? Can it adjust to differences among users in their needs for output and to differences from one time to another in the output needs of an individual user?

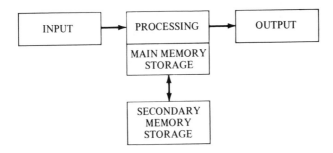

Figure 1.3   Functional view of the computer system.

Processing and storage characteristics will determine some of the user friendliness of input and output, such as how quickly the system responds, so there is an indirect impact. There is also a more direct impact of processing and storage on user friendliness. Because data processing technical staff, known as *DPers*, are in short supply in the work force, responsibility is being given to non-DP staff, also called *end-users*, to establish processing and storage methods in their own systems. When this happens, it isn't only a matter of the capabilities and limitations of processing and storage, but also a matter of how easily the end-user can exploit the capabilities and avoid the limitations.

Another way to view the computer system is from the perspective of component types. The two traditionally recognized components are hardware and software. *Hardware* consists of the computer machinery—the electronic, magnetic, and electromechanical devices that carry out the various system functions. Keyboards are input hardware. So are the different types of optical character recognition equipment that read labels when a grocery store customer is checking out at a cash register or when a department store employee is taking an inventory of items on the shelves.

Processing hardware includes the CPU and main memory devices. Output hardware includes printer, CRT terminals, and other devices for putting information into human-readable form. *CRT* stands for cathode ray tube, which is the TV-like tube on what is becoming a common office fixture. Calling it a *terminal* means it is an input or output device. In this case, the keyboard is input hardware and the cathode ray tube is output hardware. Another name for the CRT terminal is *VDT* (video display terminal). Because some terminals have video displays employing technologies other than the cathode ray tube, VDT is a good way to refer to this entire group of devices with keyboards and screens.

Secondary memory hardware includes the equipment for writing onto secondary memory media and reading from them. Magnetic tape drives write onto and read from magnetic tapes. Magnetic disk drives do the same for magnetic disks. Card punches and card readers do the same for paper cards.

The *software* component of the computer system consists of the instructions telling the hardware what to do. The CPU performs arithmetic operations and logical operations and coordinates actions of other parts of the system. But it is the software that tells the CPU which particular arithmetic and logical operations you want it to perform and how you want it to coordinate the system. If you imagine the hardware to be a record player, then the grooves on the phonograph record are the software. If you imagine the hardware to be a player piano, then the holes on the music roll are the software. Because software is stored on something, the tape or disk with the instructions on it is often referred to as software.

When counting computer system components, many users think only of the hardware and the software. But people who use those systems to help in decision making realize there is another important component—the information. A classic data processing motto is GIGO (*G*arbage *I*n, *G*arbage *O*ut). Even with the finest hardware and software, the computer system will spew out garbage if all you put into it is garbage. It is the task of the processing step to purify the input by, for instance, calculating averages and trend lines to cancel out random errors in the data. But, clearly, the more polluted the input, the more polluted the output.

There are three major sources of information for the computer system. First, you can collect the information yourself or assign others within your organization to collect it specifically for you. Secondly, you can use information already collected in other places in your organization. This is called using a *data base*.

The third source for information includes organizations outside your own that you pay to provide facts in computer-readable form on request. With these commercial data bases, also called *data banks*, there are enough different types of information to meet a great variety of organizational needs.

Being parts of the same system, hardware, software, and information characteristics are interrelated. Software takes account of the peculiarities of the hardware; if special circuitry allows a request to be processed much faster when requested in a specific way, the software should use that specific way. Information takes account of the limitations of the hardware and software; it makes no sense to plan to store records concerning 100,000 different kinds of items in inventory if there isn't sufficient memory space in the hardware or if you don't have a hardware–software combination allowing quick access to the records.

Figure 1.4 diagrams the two-way influences between hardware, software, and information. Notice that Figure 1.4 also contains a fourth component—people. A system is usually part of a larger system, and in this case, the computer system is valuable because it is a major part of the computerized decision making system. This larger system includes as a component the users who interrelate with the hardware, software, and information, and it is

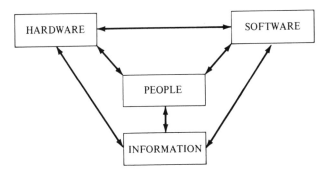

Figure 1.4 Components of the computerized decision making system.

the nature of these interrelationships involving people that determines the degree of computer system user friendliness.

Consider, for instance, that the various items of hardware called paper printers produce different-quality output. The highest-quality output is called correspondence quality, and it is similar to typewritten material. For working documents, however, there are methods of printing that are much faster and much less expensive, although the output resembles a matrix of dots rather than solid printed numbers and letters.

Suppose that the designer of a certain computerized decision making system chooses to save money by using only dot matrix printers that produce only working-document-quality output. The people in the system, the users, might find themselves having to arrange for secretaries to type reports before submitting the reports to other offices because people in those other offices expect correspondence quality. The system would be more user friendly if correspondence-quality hardware were made available to the people in the system so they could avoid the extra typing.

But it could work the other way around as well. The arrows between people and hardware go both ways, for in the well-functioning system, hardware characteristics influence people characteristics. Another possible outcome in the dot matrix printing example is that employees throughout the organization decide it is worthwhile to save some money by using working-document-quality instead of correspondence-quality output whenever possible.

Because different people in the organization have different needs and because the same person has different needs at different times, component flexibility is crucial. This is especially true in the people–information interface. Most managers at most times want summarized information without excessive details. However, if the summarizing is done over time, some of the information will necessarily be old. There are circumstances in which a decision maker wants only the latest facts, even if this means getting into details. The user-friendly system provides summarized historical information, detailed up-to-the-moment information, and various shades in-between.

Managers rightfully demand user friendliness, as does the marketplace, simply because it is possible. When one company makes user-friendly system components, others will start making them too so they can stay in business. What makes user friendliness possible is the *microchip*. On the chip, which is a piece of semiconductor material no bigger than a fingernail, can be packaged all sorts of simple and complicated arithmetic and logic routines. The microchip is a CPU, a central processing unit. The capabilities of one chip often exceed those of CPUs in early computer models that filled an entire room.

When you've a CPU that fits on a chip, a cycle, illustrated in Figure 1.5, begins to spiral upward. The cycle starts with smart computers being small enough to easily fit on any desk. Then when employees consider the help offered by these readily available tools, they want them. As increasing numbers of people in increasing numbers of organizations order up computers, it costs less to make and market each computer because of the economies of mass production and volume sales. The spiral continues with mass production of hardware creating a market for software to meet all types of managerial needs. Even if you're a cemetery owner wanting software to help you out in space planning, there are soon enough others in your profession with your needs for some enterprising programmer to create the right software. The circle is completed as lower prices for hardware and a higher variety of software lead to even more people wanting computers in their offices.

This is one way the chip pushes for user friendliness. With more computers in offices, there is a ready market for hardware, software, and information components that staff can easily learn to use, that provide answers quickly and reliably, and that adjust to the user's style of making decisions. There is also a more direct push from the chip. Microchips are now built to be used in a variety of ways in different computer systems. This means the CPU operations can be readily individualized, and when any system component is designed to meet your particular needs, that component is automatically more user friendly.

The chip helps other system components fit better with the people. There are also computer system devices that pressure the people to make the changes. A good example is an output method called the microfiche. A microfiche is a piece of film about the size of an index card. It is capable of holding the images of a few hundred pages of typewriter paper. A common use of microfiche is in public libraries, where endless rows of catalog files can be replaced by the equivalent of a shoe box filled with fiche.

Managers have a love–hate relationship with microfiche. The part of the manager's brain considering costs loves fiche. Compared to paper, fiche can be printed faster by the computer, takes up less storage space, and costs less

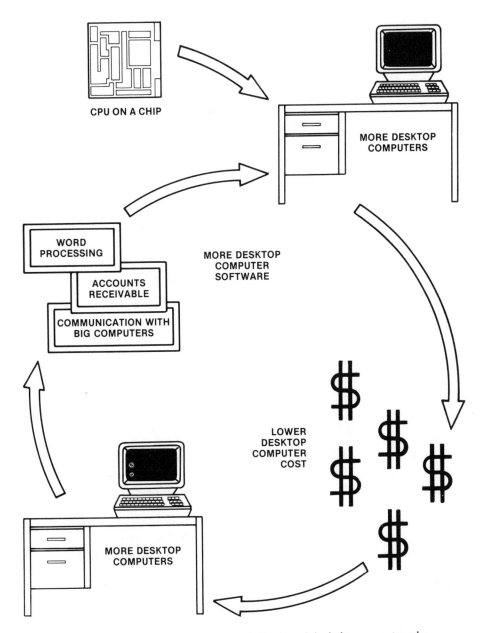

CPU ON A CHIP

MORE DESKTOP COMPUTERS

WORD PROCESSING

ACCOUNTS RECEIVABLE

COMMUNICATION WITH BIG COMPUTERS

MORE DESKTOP COMPUTER SOFTWARE

LOWER DESKTOP COMPUTER COST

MORE DESKTOP COMPUTERS

Figure 1.5 How the microchip leads to spiraling growth in desktop computer sales.

to duplicate from originals. But the part of the manager's brain concerned with gathering information frequently hates using fiche. For one thing, in spite of the small size, it is actually less portable than paper if you figure in the TV-sized machine required to read from the fiche.

When it's on the reader, problems might have only begun. Once you get the image in focus, you notice that you've placed the fiche upside down or wrongside up. You reinsert the fiche, and as you move the image across the screen, trying to find the desired page of material, the blur forces you to look away.

The problems in visually scanning fiche are related to another issue. Skilled decision makers like to get the big picture. Because they don't want to miss seeing the forest with undue focus on the trees, they often spread computer paper printouts all over the desks and mentally, as well as visually, scan the information. This isn't possible with fiche when the reader provides images of only one or two pages at a time.

Fiche also causes security concerns. The image might not be portable, but the fiche certainly is. As any respectable spy or fan of spy movies knows, it's always easier to remove fiche than paper documents from an office. The content need not be government defense secrets. Amateur industrial spies can find a market for lists of good business customers, sales figures, or mailing lists. Once off the company premises, the thief can quickly and inexpensively reproduce the fiche and then later return it to the unsuspecting organization. It also isn't too difficult to alter the information on a fiche and then replace the genuine with the bogus copy.

There are ways of overcoming, or at least addressing, these problems. Microfiche readers can be purchased that allow the image to be rotated on the screen so the fiche itself doesn't have to be repositioned. Systems of Computer-Aided Retrieval, or CAR, are expensive, but they allow quick access to a specific document in a large file without the bother of screen blur. Paper copies can be made from fiche for those who want to spread the wealth of records around themselves.

You can establish special security measures to make it less likely fiche will be stolen, or for that matter accidentally lost, which is another problem that comes with the small size. Where loss or theft are special problems, microfilm can be a better choice than microfiche. It is somewhat more difficult to steal the roll of film, and alterations on the film are somewhat easier to detect.

Overall, the best way to address the problems is to identify the capabilities and limitations of the technology in your particular applications. Many organizations find fiche best for archival storage—the long-term storage of records where viewing might be required someday. In these cases, records consulted frequently are kept on low-cost secondary memory media, like magnetic tapes, with perhaps a backup copy of critical records maintained on fiche.

Other organizations find great value in the small size and ease of updating fiche. A major book distributor mails a current inventory each week to stores throughout the country. The company uses fiche because the entire set of records can be sent in one business envelope. On the receiving end, the store managers put up with the bother of fiche because of the low cost, small storage space, and information timeliness.

But do the store employees, the ones who use the fiche most often, gracefully accept the bother, or do they turn off the machine? The answer is that employees become accustomed to the technology when it has an appropriate place in the organization. The bookstore employees went through the same adjustment period we all went through when first visiting a library with a microfiche card catalog. They welcome fiche when retrieving information about a specific book, but resist using fiche in favor of paper copy when the task is comparing sales figures among a number of titles in a number of categories listed on a number of pages.

There are a few lessons from the matter of the microfiche. Chief among them is, "Try out new computer system components." If you supervise others who would be using the components, have them try it out at different times in different circumstances Be patient, for the best methods may demand adjustments from the people component, you and your staff. Look for flexibility in the method, but remember that even the best improvements rarely replace completely the present methods. There is certainly a role for paper output alongside microfiche output, and certainly a role for regular old typewriters alongside word processors with their microchips.

If after a time it is clear that too many adjustments would be demanded of the people or it is unclear what place this component would have in the overall decision making system, move on. There are too many user-friendly components on the market now for you to be burdened with user-aversive ones. And if you move on, keep the willingness to try out components. With this idea of trying it out, you'll develop within yourself and your co-workers a spirit of experimentation invaluable for these days when computer system technologies are changing so quickly.

Chapter 2

The Natural Incompatibility of Manager and Machine

You'd think they'd take this fool machine
And pull it out to sell it.
It never does quite what we want
But only what we tell it.

People and computers think differently, and it is with the proper blending of the differing styles that quality decisions occur. Computers are at their best with routine, repetitive tasks. People are at their best with tasks that involve change. When presented routine, repetitive tasks, people at first improve performance skills as they gain experience. But then they become less accurate and less thorough as further repetition produces boredom.

Computer systems handle decision making and other complex tasks by going through a series of discrete steps performed in a strict sequence. People often make decisions in this same way, using checklists, for example. Still, most people find it better to handle decisions in a series of interacting steps that spiral toward a solution rather than move toward it in a straight line.

First a broad overall policy decision is made or one part of the overall decision is made tentatively. Next the effects of the decision are observed, and it is seen how the effects interact with other decisions. Then another cycle of decisions is made that comes closer to solving the problem. In this process, people use great amounts of intuition and creativity, both of which are not often found within computer systems.

Beyond this, employees must handle factors that computers handle poorly, if at all. Chief among these is organizational politics. Decisions that are otherwise excellent often fail to gain acceptance because not enough attention was devoted to who has influence with whom and who favors what in the organization. A computer system can take into account only the kinds of information stored inside its memory, and staff members aren't likely to put inside computer memory information about organizational politics. They carry such things inside their heads, where the chance of embarrassing disclosure is less than when these things are recorded inside the computer.

In addition, power relationships and personal preferences change quickly and are often revealed by sources with only moderate reliability. The skilled manager combines these sorts of soft information with the structured information coming out of the computers. The manager who fails to appreciate the differences in these information types won't get the best from that output.

Also important in getting the best is appreciating that your decision making style differs from that of some others and that, within yourself, your decision making style differs from one time to the next. Sometimes you prefer your information in the form of words, at other times in the form of numbers, at other times in the form of graphics or pictures, and at many times, if the cost is not too high, in the form of all three. Related to this, some computer systems differ in the quality of words and graphics produced and the ease with which they are produced.

The level of detail is another distinguishing factor. Sometimes you want quite detailed data, such as daily inventory status or weekly sales figures for each item number. Most of the time, however, people fear being buried in details and they aim for the overall view, such as quarterly sales figures by general item classification.

A major determinant of the type of output desired is the type of decision. Management scientists divide the decisions you make into three categories: operational control, management control, and strategic planning.

Operational control decisions are the type you make routinely and repetitively. Deciding how many overtime hours are needed next week and choosing employees to work those hours are operational control decisions. Other examples include selecting a route and carrier for a particular shipment and ordering raw materials. Operational control decisions usually have a short time span. However, some of them, such as deciding when to do preventive maintenance on equipment, can extend over a longer period.

Operational control decisions are prime candidates for automation. The input factors, like current raw materials inventory or time since last maintenance, are clear-cut, and given the proper input, computers can make the operational control decisions.

At the other extreme are *strategic planning* decisions. These are the long-range decisions in which considerable organizational resources are at risk. If your organization decides to offer a new product or service to clients or customers, this would probably involve commitment of money and personnel over a period of time. Strategic planning decisions occur regarding the purchase of a major item of equipment, such as die production machinery by

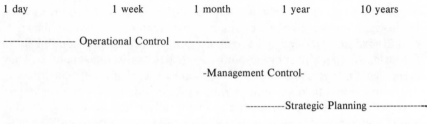

Figure 2.1. Relative time spans of operational control, management control, and strategic planning decisions.

a manufacturing plant, a Computerized Axial Tomography device by a medical center, or for that matter, a million-dollar computer system by any organization.

Strategic planning decisions provide overall direction to the organization's endeavors and limit the alternatives for choices made later. As a result, these types of decisions are often made only by senior managers. Still, employees at any level can be asked to recommend strategic planning actions to the senior managers. It is therefore important for any employee to appreciate the role computer systems play in strategic planning decisions.

Actually, that role is often limited. Because of the extended time frame and the large number of changeable factors involved, strategic planning decisions require the spiraling process in which computers are so weak. One family of data processing tools, called decision support systems, are designed to provide to managers information in a form best suited to the characteristics of strategic planning. However, a much higher percentage of each operational control than each strategic planning decision will be handled by computers. Many organizations have been seriously impaired because they depended too much upon computer output for strategic planning.

Management control decisions have characteristics between operational control and strategic planning. They are made regularly, but not routinely. Establishment of pay grades and training schedules are management control decisions, as are decisions about marketing strategies for an existing product or service line. An important distinction between management control and strategic planning decisions is that the time frame of the former often allows the results to be observed in time for the next round of decisions of that type. The true results of strategic planning decisions, on the other hand, often aren't known for many years.

Figure 2.1 diagrams the relative time spans involved in the three decision types. As is seen there, wide variations exist within each type and the time spans overlap.

Because the results of a management control decision frequently are known before the next round of that decision type, the system user can sharpen up the mix of computerized and noncomputerized elements.

Management control decisions are therefore candidates for at least partial automation if the user keeps in mind the necessity of mixing in the other elements and revising the mix over time.

For instance, a major part of establishing salary schedules can be done by computerized analysis of salaries received by workers in equivalent jobs both inside and outside the organization, with corrections applied to this analysis to take account of the number of available applicants and cost of living indexes for the employment area. But computer processing is only part of it. Human beings first need to define what constitutes equivalent job titles and need to approve the formulas used in the corrections.

Computer processing, then, has the greatest role to play in operational control decisions and a lesser, but important, role in management control decisions.

The advantages of computer processing over human decision making include speed, precision, and memory capacity. The speed of computers allows people to take advantage of opportunities quickly, such as changing investment strategies in cash management based upon analysis of market conditions. The precision of computers allows users to predict trends based upon minimum amounts of information. With the massive memory offered by the computer, the precision lets the user see exceptions from general trends. The massive memory also helps when the user must review simultaneous interrelationships among a number of factors.

At the same time, employing computers in decision making can cause problems. One set of problems comes from the pressure to quantify. Because computers traditionally deal with numbers, there is a pressure from those working with computers to put a number onto everything. But many factors important in decision making cannot be quantified exactly. You measure them in terms of more versus less or sooner versus later, and to go beyond that is a misleading exactness. When you encounter considerations like corporate social responsibility, it's best to view them in terms of broad limits rather than precise numbers.

An advantage of computer processing is called number crunching. This refers to the ability of the system to average together large amounts of data so that the averages will have more certainty than each of the individual cases. Classical examples are the mortality tables used by life insurance companies. A life insurance company does not know the precise day upon which a particular person will die. Yet by averaging together mortality data on large numbers of individuals, the company can establish insurance premiums that are low enough to attract customers while high enough to protect the company from unacceptable levels of risk.

Whatever type of organization you work for, your organization takes risks. When it commits money, staff, or materials to one alternative, it limits its ability to commit to other alternatives. This is most true with strategic planning decisions, but also is true with even operational control decisions. In selecting a particular route and carrier for a shipment, as an example, your organization is taking a risk. When you collect information on the results of shipments with that carrier and others, a computer system can quickly number crunch to calculate the average performance of each carrier, in that way allowing you to reduce the amount of risk.

Still, averages can have a misleading accuracy because it depends upon what you include in each average. There is the story of the judge who, at his retirement dinner, was bragging that on average he had done very well throughout his career. He was quite confident, he said, that for every innocent person he had condemned to death, there was a guilty person he had let go free.

The judge's average rate of convictions may have been in accord with the average rate of guilt in the population he dealt with, but this isn't something you measure by averages.

Similarly, there often are times that your best course of action is to look over the averages that appear in the computer output and then get out into the field to do individual observations. To see how to increase money your organization makes, look over sales figure averages and then go out on sales calls. To see how to save money, look at a computer-formatted cost center budget and then observe how the product is being manufactured or the service is being provided. Averages might tell you what the trouble spots are, but a good case study tells you why those spots are trouble.

Averages aside, the precision of computer output can mislead the decision maker. This point is illustrated by the tale of the computer programmer who decided to pose a riddle to the new sophisticated interactive computer system. His riddle concerned analog watches, which, unlike digital watches, have hour and minute hands.

"Is it better," asked the programmer, "to have an analog watch that has stopped completely or one that loses precisely two seconds each day?"

The computer system responded immediately. "IT IS SUBSTANTIALLY BETTER TO HAVE AN ANALOG WATCH THAT HAS STOPPED COMPLETELY."

Since this was a sophisticated interactive system, the programmer was able to pose a follow-up query: "Why?"

Again the computer responded immediately. "BECAUSE," read the message, "AN ANALOG WATCH THAT HAS STOPPED COMPLETELY WILL BE EXACTLY RIGHT TWICE EACH DAY. HOWEVER, AN ANALOG WATCH THAT LOSES PRECISELY TWO SECONDS PER DAY WILL BE EXACTLY RIGHT ONLY ONCE EVERY 59.18 YEARS."

As a decision maker, you do not want that sort of exactness, but it is what the computer system will provide you unless programmed otherwise. Managing by the numbers alone can be suicidal for an organization.

Another set of problems comes from computer output disrupting the user's sense of timing. On one hand, the output can pressure the user to act too soon. Because of the speed with which computers take in information, process it, and put out the results, users may act before the time is correct.

The time may be wrong because the situation is not ripe for action. If negotiating is involved, it may be better to encourage the other party to make the first move, even though you've complete computer output regarding the matter. If there's a problem, any action may actually be premature action because many problems work out with no intervention by a particular employee.

With speedy, detailed output from a computer system, too many staff members forget their good managerial common sense, saying to themselves, "I have all the information. I'll do it myself." In doing it yourself, you're likely to cheat yourself of time and your subordinates of the opportunity for self-development. Don't allow the computer system to pressure you into acting prematurely.

The other side of the timing issue is information overload. Computers can spew out paper, and that amount of paper can immobilize decision makers. Bad managers hide behind the paper. They say they must review all the paper before making a decision because they are afraid of making a decision. Good, conscientious managers can be misled into thinking better decisions will result from a complete review of all available output.

The truth is that there is never enough time to look through all available output. As a decision maker you are paid to act on the basis of incomplete information. You are paid to take risks. You are paid to use your intuition, for there is never enough time to look through it all.

Actually most employees realized this before the computers came, but many have forgotten it. Just as you can muff an opportunity by acting too early, you can miss an opportunity by acting too late. Remember that an essential part of a good decision is timing.

One way to make information overload less likely is to be selective in consulting the data base. Knowing when to shut off or discard output helps in blending of DP and non-DP decision making. Appreciating the differing styles also helps. For long-range decisions or decisions made when the input factors are unclear, don't depend excessively upon computer analysis. For routine, repetitive decisions involving mostly numbers, see how much of the work can be off-loaded to computer systems. In every kind of decision, include the qualitative factors and, above all, view the machine as electronic servant, not as all-knowing master.

Chapter 3

Messages for the People

Along with variety, people love action. They will use computers only if they can learn their use quickly. Some computer vendors tell sales staff that they've only forty minutes in which to demonstrate the value of the component to the non-DPer because after forty minutes, the prospective customer's mind will want to move on. Actually the total limit is probably longer than forty minutes, especially with return sales calls. Still, there is a real limit.

A comparison can be made to learning a game, whether it be racquetball or backgammon. Most people want to learn the basics and then begin developing skills, even if it takes some time to master all the refinements of the game. Your racquetball coach might argue that you should learn the basics well and then build on them, for you might form bad habits by taking on too much too soon. Yet even if you agree with the wisdom of this view, you're probably going to try out some fancy maneuvers when the coach isn't looking. In the same way, even when employees see the need to take time mastering all the capabilities of a computer system, they want to start using the basics as soon as possible, and they are likely to try out more complicated system functions before completely mastering the simpler ones.

With computers, the rules of the game are expressed in terms of the *command language*. The command language consists of the set of words and terms you use to communicate with the CPU. If you sit down at a computer terminal and type onto the keyboard, "Print the current budget for the Purchasing Department," the words "Print," "current," "Purchasing," and so on are part of the command language.

Right off, the system is easier to start using when the command language resembles English. It works out better if you can type in "Print" rather than have to enter some abbreviation such as "Pnt" or some code such as "4." The system may ignore some of the letters you enter. From the standpoint of system engineering, it takes up less space on the screen and in computer memory for you to enter "Pnt," which is three characters of information rather than "Print," which if five. The unit is the *byte*, which is equivalent to one digit, letter, or symbol. The number "7531" takes up four bytes because it is four digits, "Pnt" takes up three bytes because it is three letters, and "Print" takes up five bytes because it is five letters in length.

This is a case where the computer operates less efficiently from the standpoint of physical engineering, but more efficiently from the standpoint of human engineering because humans prefer to be able to use English-like messages in communicating with the computer. It is worth taking up the extra bytes if this makes it easier for novices to learn to use the system.

In reality, the system is programmed to still operate quite efficiently. When you type in "Print," the system can temporarily record the five bytes, but then quickly translate them into a code that occupies only two or three bytes to represent that command. The system might not even wait for you to finish typing in a response. If the system poses a "Yes–No" question to you, you might find that there is a response after you type in the "Y" or the "N" without the system giving you a chance to finish your word.

This can be a minor annoyance. It's like a co-worker asking you a question and then interrupting you before you finish your answer. But if you think about the computer's response in terms of you getting a faster answer and in terms of saving yourself the trouble of typing in needless letters, it makes it easier to endure.

The system ignores words as well as letters for purposes of user friendliness. In "Print the current budget for the Purchasing Department," the computer disregards a few of the words. You could just as well, and more efficiently in the view of systems engineers, have typed in, "Print current budget Purchasing." But that is less like English, so acceptance of the system is more likely when the system is more tolerant.

As you become more experienced, you'll no doubt find yourself typing in "Y" instead of "Yes" and "Print current budget Purchasing" instead of "Print the current budget for the Purchasing Department" because you will want to save yourself and the system time and motion. But the best computers allow you to take the long way around if that is the more comfortable route for now.

A particular nuisance for end-users is inconsistencies among command languages. Suppose that you want a copy of some output. It is a bother if one software package requires you to type in "Print" to accomplish this task, but another package accepts only the command "Report." Often the different software programs in a system were written by different people at different times. The result of this may be that you use one set of words and procedures when requesting information from computer memory, another set for

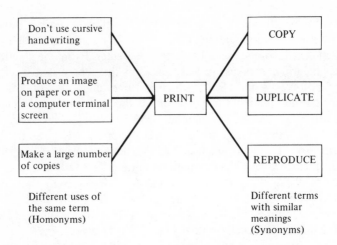

Figure 3.1 Examples of homonyms and synonyms.

equivalent commands when updating, and still another set for security operations.

When evaluating software packages to add to packages you already have, consider whether different terms must be used in the new and old packages to accomplish the same sorts of tasks. If the new package is superior to the existing one in many ways, it is probably worth learning the new vocabulary. If the new package is not clearly superior to the existing one, the new language may be a substantial bother.

Correspondingly, the problem for system designers is to create command languages that allow the end-user to employ English-like terms, but that avoid the ambiguities of English. Our natural language allows us to use different words for the same idea. I may say, "Copy the form," or "Duplicate the form," and the person I'm talking to knows I mean the same thing.

Then, too, the same word can have many different meanings. A manager is talking about your budget. What does he mean by "budget"? Budget can refer to the amount of money you were allocated to spend at the start of the fiscal year. It might refer to the amount you were allocated to spend at the start of the calendar quarter. Does he mean the amount of money you have left to spend this year or this calendar quarter? Perhaps he means a document in a line budget format or in a program budget format. "Budget" can have these and other meanings.

Figure 3.1 illustrates the two types of ambiguity. In ways that differ somewhat from the common definitions in English grammar, *synonyms* in data processing are different terms having similar meanings and *homonyms* are instances in which the same term is used in different ways.

When people deal with other people, the meaning of a homonym is obtained from the context in which the term is used. If I request of my administrative assistant a comparison of the sales figures for California and New York, my assistant realizes I mean the State of New York, and when I want a comparison of New York with Dallas, my assistant assumes I mean New York City. If I talk about "invoice" with reference to accounts payable, my meaning is understood to be different than if I use the word in talking with somebody regarding accounts receivable.

Because people can make these kinds of translations, employees find it easier to use shorthand and terms that first come to mind rather than searching for just the right word or explaining every aspect of what is meant. In addition, there are times workers are intentionally ambiguous. Negotiating often requires terms that could be interpreted in a few different ways so that a broad area can be created for agreement. Then, as part of the negotiations, the meaning of the terms is made more precise.

For these reasons, people quickly get into habits of using somewhat ambiguous language. The problem for designers of computer systems is that data are processed most smoothly when input is unambiguous.

Some designers meet the challenge by having the system respond to ambiguous input with a message notifying the user that he or she has committed an error. More sophisticated systems request further clarification when ambiguity is detected. A good command language communicates to the user the limitations of the system, eliminating questions the computer system should not legitimately answer. The command language might not allow you to ask, "What is our best marketing strategy for next year?" because an answer would require the intuition, creativity, and value judgments associated with human decision making.

Another method for reducing ambiguity in user commands is to have the system present a *menu* on the screen. A menu is a set of choices. For example, the system might print on the screen, "WHICH GENERAL LEDGER ROUTINE DO YOU WANT?" and then, instead of requiring you to type in the name, the system may print on the screen, "1. ACCOUNTS RECEIVABLE 2. ACCOUNTS PAYABLE 3. FIXED ASSETS. PRESS BUTTON TO INDICATE." With the menu, you don't have to recall all the alternatives that are available or recall the correct name of each alternative. It also is faster to type in the single digit than to spell out the name of the item.

Menus are especially welcomed by new users of a system. More experienced users often dislike menus. There are two reasons for their displeasure. First, when the number of alternative responses is great, there may not be room on the screen to list them all, so the less popular alternatives won't be included. With menus, then, there are times when a user isn't aware of all the capabilities of the system.

This objection is less likely when decision-tree menus or branching schemes are employed. Here the first menu has very general categories and then, depending upon the choice made, progressively more detailed menus are presented. An early screen might list seven or eight major types of routines available. When you indicated the type of routine, the screen might show seven or eight choices within that type. Great numbers of alternatives can be included in the menu repertoire with the branching scheme, for only a limited number are included on the screen at once.

That leads to the second objection experienced users have to menus. You may find yourself going through many levels of branching to get to what you want. This is acceptable if it helps reveal to you the unknown capabilities of the system, but when you know what is available and know exactly what you desire, having to go through menus is a bother. People experienced with a system like to be able to shortcut the menu.

Seek systems that provide both good branching menus and opportunities for shortcuts. A shortcut might be the user simply typing in the title of what is desired. It might be a matter of employing a *default option*. A default option tells the software to make a decision. For instance, instead of stating the size of paper you want a report printed on, you might leave a blank on the screen or the entry form. The system might then select the most popular paper size, such as 8½ by 11 inches, without you having to take the time to type that in or select it from the menu.

When typing in material, *format prompts* are useful. Format prompts are cues as to the correct physical arrangement of the information. Suppose the system requests you to enter a date. The format prompt might read, "USE NUMBERS. MM/DD/YYYY." There are many ways to enter a date. The prompt tells you to use a number rather than an alphabetic abbreviation for the month, divide the three parts of the entry with slash marks, and enter year as four digits. Few users, even very experienced ones, object to format prompts unless the prompts occupy so much space on the screen that commands have to be entered on a series of screens rather than just one.

Most of all, however, users like systems that help them deal competently with errors. After making a mistake, the user wants to know, "What do I do now?" Error messages that appear on the screen should concentrate on helping the user determine this next step to take.

Often the best step to take next is to step back. That is, the system should allow the user to withdraw an action just taken, canceling out that action. This is the equivalent of letting the user withdraw from a blind alley in a maze. Seek system routines that include this undo mode. Avoid systems that, in response to an error, destroy valid information already entered or force you to start the input task all over again.

With error messages, there can be significance in seemingly minor matters, such as whether the message is in all capital letters or in both upper- and lower-case letters. Even the kindest error message makes the offender feel a little bit like an idiot, and it simply is easier to accept, "You idiot," than, "YOU IDIOT." Regardless of the words in the error message, upper- and lower-case letters are generally better than all upper-case letters.

A chief exception to this rule would be the instance where a user has committed some terrible sin, such as ordering the system to needlessly launch a nuclear missile or erase the computer's memory of your oganization's best customers. In these cases, error messages should be in all capital letters, the messages should flash brightly, and bells should ring.

Because end-users like to feel competent and primarily want to know, "What do I do next?" they get irritated at messages that go into great detail about what they did wrong and why it was wrong. Few things are more frustrating to an action-oriented manager than having to go through a lesson about the computer system's peculiarities when in the middle of getting a job done. After a few such experiences, those action-oriented managers—who tend to be the best managers—will give up on the system.

Still, at some point broader knowledge about the system is needed so that the end-uses don't keep making the same kinds of mistakes and so the users recognize the system's capabilities. Seminars and workshops can help, especially when accompanied by good learning materials.

User manuals are part of this package of learning materials. User manuals tell you how to operate the computer as a tool in your decision making and how to correct errors. User manuals and other learning materials should incorporate principles of adult learning. Actually, the principles of learning are similar for adults and children. One important difference is that adults are less willing than children to learn without evidence of a clear application to everyday life.

User manuals should focus sharply on just what the end-user needs to know to employ the system and avoid errors. Too often, user manuals contain technical material that is of little use, and so of little interest, to the end-user. A mistake made even more often is assuming that the end-user will read the manual from beginning to end in that order and will try out complex system functions only after simple functions have been mastered completely. In reality, people rarely read through the manual completely or in perfectly proper sequence, and they use the manual in different ways at different times.

When correcting errors, they will try to quickly find the section that tells them what to do now. Good user manuals, then, have a diagnostic chart with page references for particular types of errors. Perhaps the screen will read, "ERROR 152," and the user manual will then have a section on errors indexed by number. It is better if the system itself produces a helpful error message on the screen, such as, "CUSTOMER NUMBER ENTERED INCORRECTLY," but with small systems, there sometimes isn't enough memory space or processing power to go beyond "ERROR 152" messages.

A person uses the manual in another way when learning about the system. Here the non-DPer is likely to browse through the material, turning on the computer and trying out functions along the way. Since you may come to important material from a variety of approaches and may skip over material that looks difficult, important points should be repeated a few times within the manual in different places and in different words. In addition, because you will try out complex functions even before simpler ones are mastered, the manual should tell you how to step back from errors you've made.

Repetition of the material makes user manuals longer. A thick, heavy manual might intimidate a user when he or she first looks at it and lifts it up. But the novice will quickly be reassured by the length if this means that explanations within the manual are conducted patiently, and it is easy to find desired material through a comprehensive index.

Actually, heavy user manuals are becoming less common. The information in the manual, including the index, can be placed inside computer memory instead of on paper, and the user can access the correct material for the situation with the speed of computer processing. Many systems have Help buttons or Help routines. If you do want an explanation of why the system is performing in certain ways or why the system believes you've committed and error, you press the Help button or type in the word "Help." The computer then accesses some relevant information and prints it on the screen for you to review.

Understanding messages, whether manuals or on the terminal screen, is easier when the messages contain simple words in short sentences. The user prefers to be told what to do instead of what not to do. If a sequence of actions is to be taken, the order of the words should correspond to the intended order of actions. For instance, the message, "Type the store code and then press the Enter key," is better than, "Press the Enter key after typing in the store code."

You might very well not have responsibility for writing user manuals or creating screen messages. The importance of these factors, however, is still there. Try out the system components, including user manuals and help screens. Intentionally make some errors, and see how the system responds and how comfortable the error routines are.

There are still other characteristics of human information processing with important implications for system design. For one thing, people like variety, but not unpredictability. This is especially true regarding system response times. When making a request, you probably like to know how long it will take for the reply to appear. Users soon learn that different sorts of requests involve different sorts of response times. A request for information stored on a magnetic tape might take 90 seconds to satisfy, but a request to correct an error on a terminal screen might involve just a second. Time of day also can make a difference. Action-oriented staff members may come to the office early or stay late because the computers respond much more quickly during those periods than at midday, when many others are entering requests, but for a particular type of request made at a particular time of day, the user expects predictability.

This can have the unexpected angle of users actually being happier with longer response times. That is, there are users who would, consciously or unconsciously, prefer to have a predictable 20-second response time than a response time varying between 2 and 22 seconds with an average of 12 seconds. Knowing it will be 20 seconds lets you turn your attention to something else briefly, but the unpredictability can cause you to start staring at the screen after 2 seconds and continue staring for as long as the full 22-second mark.

Expanding the capacity of the system with more hardware and software can even-out response times. But demand upon computer systems seems to always stay at least a little bit beyond system capacity regardless of that capacity. Some experts in the human design of computer systems have suggested holding back quick responses so there is more predictability. A less extreme, and more interesting, option is to have a countdown clock on the screen that reflects an estimate of how long the system will take to reply. The manager then doesn't have to wait in suspense. At the least, the system should provide to the user some acknowledgement that the request was received. One bother of a long, unpredictable response time is the concern that the message didn't get through.

Similarly, when the manager makes a complex request of the system, it works out well if the system gives partial responses along the way. On the other side, if the system is requesting long or complicated entries, it's best if the system digests and acknowledges the entries one piece at a time. If weekly client results are to be entered for a one-year period, the system might request the January figures, produce a message saying the January figures have been received, request the February figures, and so on.

The technical term for this idea is closure, which means presenting complex or long tasks in a series of segments with a message of completion after each segment. In having command languages consistent across software packages, in having the computer system handle ambiguity, in having good error routines, and in aiming for predictable response times, you are reducing the feelings of suspense for you and for your co-workers. You are letting yourself and the others quickly get the idea and get on with it. The underlying principle is that business people love action but, aside from Alfred Hitchcock movies, high-stakes negotiations, and a few other activities, business people hate suspense.

Chapter 4

The Terminally Well Organization

Choose your video display terminal with care. The VDT is the single most important item of hardware in your computerized decision making system. For one thing, you'll be using this terminal very often to get information from the data base. If there's glare on the screen or if you can't position the screen and keyboard in comfortable ways at the same time or if you keep hitting the wrong key while hitting the intended key, you'll probably shut off the terminal and try getting your information in other ways.

When that happens, resources expended by your organization to develop and maintain the computer system have been wasted. There is an additional, perhaps even greater, cost. In turning off the terminal, you're failing to use a powerful management tool, so your organization won't save money or make money as well as it could.

VDTs are being used with such frequency because of the trend away from batch retrieval and toward on-line retrieval. With batch, the older method, you submit a request for information to the people in a data center. Your request is processed in turn, and the information is sent back to you hours, perhaps even days, later. You might make your query by having a clerk punch it onto a card that can be read by input hardware. The method is called *batch processing* because your query, or job, is batched together with many other jobs and the batch is then entered into the CPU. With one type of batch processing, called RJE for Remote Job Entry, jobs are stored on secondary memory media, like magnetic tapes, and the entire batch of jobs is then sent all at once to the main CPU in the form of electronic signals over telephone lines, cable, or microwave channels.

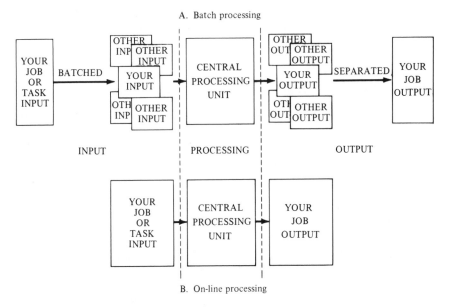

Figure 4.1   Batch processing compared to on-line processing.

As you see in Figure 4.1A, the output as well as the input of batch processing is a collection of jobs. In the case of output, the jobs then need to be separated.

The advantage of batch processing is that more efficient use is made of available equipment. The work load can be evened-out because the people operating the computers can wait until the machinery is free before entering new tasks. That is also the disadvantage of batch processing. Operators can wait for a more convenient time, but the decision makers have to wait to get answers to their questions. The problem is that skilled decision makers hate waiting. They want to get answers and move ahead.

As the price of computer hardware dropped and as more tasks could be handled by the same priced equipment, on-line processing became more popular. On-line aims for effective, rather than efficient, use of the system components. With *on-line processing*, diagrammed in Figure 4.1B, you enter your request more or less directly into the CPU and your request is answered as soon as the CPU is available. You're able to retrieve infomation in seconds or minutes rather than hours or days. The VDT replaced the keypunch machine, and more users queried the data base themselves rather than going through a clerk or secretary. For making out paychecks and other repetitive chores, batch processing remains the cost-effective mode. For situations where information is needed quickly by decision makers, on-line is the method of choice.

With the movement toward on-line and the development of the microchip, other changes occurred that make selection of the right VDT critical. These changes concern the terminal's editing and formatting capabilities. Even with the price of computing power going down, operating a large CPU is expensive. Often it makes sense to have a VDT do certain jobs itself.

One type of task where this is true is *editing*. Editing means making corrections in input. If you hit the wrong key in typing a word into the terminal, the terminal should itself contain the circuits that allow you to correct your mistake. That is too trivial a matter for bothering a large CPU. Similarly, if you want to change the sequence of numbers you've typed in, the terminal should allow you to do this without requiring typing of the entire series or use of a large CPU.

One meaning of *formatting* is the physical arrangement of output on the printed page or on the terminal screen. If you rearrange numbers in rows instead of columns, that is a change in format. If you take text that is single spaced with the first word of each paragraph indented, and you arrange it as double-spaced text with no indentations for new paragraphs, those are format changes.

As with editing, it's often best to have these sorts of changes accomplished by the VDT rather than by a large, separate CPU for cost efficiencies. The same information can be provided to various managers, and each can use his or her VDT to format the information in the precise way he or she likes best.

The notion here is terminal *intelligence*. A terminal that performs editing, formatting, and other processing chores without depending upon a separate CPU is called an intelligent or a *smart terminal*. This is accomplished by building into the VDT its own small CPU in the form of a microchip.

The smart terminal can handle many chores by itself, and when contact with the larger CPU is necessary for fancier processing, work can be divided between the terminal and the larger CPU. Smart terminals make for a more reliable computer system, too. If the organization's one large CPU breaks down, certain processing can still be done using just the smart VDTs, and if one smart VDT breaks down, the work can be shifted to another.

The availability of smart terminals provides opportunities for the end-user, but also creates additional responsibilities. You pay more for a smarter terminal, so you'll be deciding how much intelligence is required. For offices in which output is formatted frequently in a variety of imaginative ways, the extra expense of terminals with sophisticated formatting capabilities is justified. In offices where data are entered repetitively in formats that change infrequently, error correction intelligence might well be all that is needed.

In those offices where data are entered repetitively, there are yet other reasons for VDT selection being important. Data entry clerks in such offices are reporting with disturbing frequency that they suffer eyestrain, headaches, backaches, and muscle fatigue after using VDTs. VDT characteristics are being discussed more often in labor union negotiations and legislative chambers. Germany, among other countries, mandates by law that VDTs meet certain human engineering standards. If you supervise employees who enter great amounts of data into a computer system, you'll be forced into concern about terminal selection.

Employee complaints began at a time when some color TV sets were believed to be emitting dangerous levels of radiation. Data entry clerks feared their monitors might be doing the same. Subsequent years of investigation by government agencies has failed to find clear evidence of excessive radiation emissions from VDTs. However, the National Institute for Occupational Safety and Health has concluded that frequent VDT use does produce physical strain.

Some of the NIOSH recommendations are, in turn, creating their own special strain for conscientious managers. NIOSH stated that employees who work intensively with VDTs should be granted a 15-minute break after every hour of screen work. They also recommended that a professional eye examination be administered to each person being considered for heavy-duty data entry, and that subsequent eye exams be given periodically to those chosen.

One response to the recommendations is to rotate job duties so that no clerk, or manager for that matter, works continuously with the VDT for hours at a time. Another response is to design VDTs in ways that reduce strain on the user. For example, all information appearing on the screen should be easy to read. Such clarity is a function of screen size, resolution, glare, brightness, and contrast.

The screen should be large enough so that the contents can be seen clearly when the terminal is placed a comfortable distance away from the user. Then the resolution on the screen should be high enough for the screen size. Information that appears crisp on a five-inch screen might appear fuzzy on a 15-inch screen because of low resolution.

Some small-system users purchase a television set to use as the output screen. When compared to a true output monitor, the TV may have an attractive cost, but it almost always has an unattractive image. On a TV, the letter "B" looks too much like the numeral "8" and a comma looks like a period. TV sets do not have enough resolution for business office use.

As bothersome as poor resolution is glare. Few business offices are designed for VDTs. Either the office was built before the computer terminals became popular or the office was built with other concerns in mind. There are windows, overhead lights, and reflective surfaces that produce glare on the VDT screen. Shop for VDTs that have glare filters. Consider placing hoods over the screens to block off offending light sources. Select terminals with screens that tilt and swivel, allowing you to position the screen in ways that avoid glare and are in other ways most comfortable. These and other user-friendly VDT features illustrated in Figure 4.2.

A common output color combination is green on a black background, which is less bothersome to the eyes over long periods than white on black.

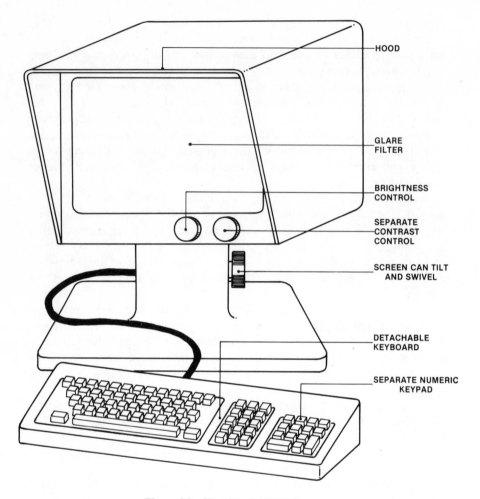

HOOD

GLARE
FILTER

BRIGHTNESS
CONTROL

SEPARATE
CONTRAST
CONTROL

SCREEN CAN TILT
AND SWIVEL

DETACHABLE
KEYBOARD

SEPARATE NUMERIC
KEYPAD

Figure 4.2   User-friendly VDT features.

Even more comfortable for the eyes is an amber foreground. Because some
VDTs using amber have a short screen life, a good warranty is especially
important with these terminals.

Of course, few contemporary computer systems restrict themselves to one
background and one foreground output color. Many terminals can display
thousands of blends of 16 basic colors. Be careful that you don't overuse
color, since multiple colors fatigue the eyes. In most situations, four colors on
a contrasting background are sufficient. The terminal that can produce
65,000 color blends might be for you and your organization an example of an
available technology not worth the money.

There are cases where multiple colors are useful. But consider whether the
system can achieve equally good results in ways that are less expensive and

less stressful for the users' eyes. Vary the intensity of the characters, with some letters and numbers brighter than others, but in the same foreground color. Use reverse video so that some material is black on a green block instead of green on a black background. Another advantage of these techniques over multicolor displays is that many users, especially males, are partially color blind.

All users, whether color blind or not, will appreciate having separate brightness and contrast controls on the VDT. The underlying theme here is the ability of the user to control output. This allows an individual employee to adjust the system to fit his or her preferred style. It also allows the individual to change system characteristics from time to time simply for the sake of change. People, unlike machines, enjoy variety and shun the routine. Thirdly, the sense of control in itself makes a computer system more user friendly.

Position the VDT screen so you can see the entire image by moving your eyes without needing to move your head. For most users and most screen sizes, this means that the screen will be 1½ to 2½ feet from your eyes. Once the screen is correctly positioned, you'll want to place the keyboard. The rule here is that your upper arms should be approximately vertical and your forearms approximately horizontal when your fingers are on the home row (a s d f j k l ;) of keys on a standard keyboard.

Getting the screen and the keyboard each in the right place at the same time is certainly easier with a keyboard that detaches from the screen unit. Unless you have the exact body dimensions of the average user for whom a one-piece unit was designed, a detachable keyboard makes life with your terminal noticeably more pleasant.

Some VDTs use in place of keys flat sheets that are touch sensitive and are marked to look like regular keyboards. Perhaps you've seen a similar technique employed on elevators in place of elevator buttons. The trouble with this on a VDT is that the user may be required to hold fingers suspended slightly above the keyboard when typing in information, touching only the desired keys. The user also is deprived of the sensory cue of knowing his or her fingers are correctly positioned on the keys.

There is one sort of situation where these membrane keypads can be valuable. This is where the terminal is in a place with much dust, many liquids, or some other substances that can get into a keyboard and gum it up. VDTs can help on the factory floor for inventory control, and rugged units with touch-sensitive membrane keypads might be the best choice.

If you do choose a membrane keypad, provide a wrist rest to make it a little more comfortable for the hands to be held in the required suspended animation. Even with a regular keyboard, a wrist rest is good.

If much of your input consists of numbers, it's convenient to have a separate numeric keypad, which resembles a calculator keyboard, rather than just the numeral keys as the top row on a standard typewriter keyboard. Most serious business terminals contain both the standard typewriter keyboard and a separate numeric keyboard.

Still another important feature is key placement, but here it is hard to provide clear specifications because managers' preferences differ. If you are accustomed to having one Shift key for upper-case letters directly to the left of the Z key and another directly to the right of the ? key, you may find it bothersome to have just one Shift key to the far left of the A key. Try out the keyboard for a long-enough period to judge if your discomfort will disappear. Also, if you like a VDT otherwise, see if improvement in your typing habits, such as arching your fingers, eliminates problems with the keyboard.

Pay attention to placement of the Control key. This is a key you depress to give other keys special control functions. For instance, instead of typing into the system, "Here is the place where I want the marked paragraph inserted," you might press the Control key and at the same time depress the A key, and this communicates the message to the CPU. It saves time and can reduce the number of errors, but it also requires acrobatic fingers when the Control key is in a clumsy location. There are advantages in having two Control keys, just as there are two Shift keys on a typewriter, and in having a lockable Control key, just as there is a Shift Lock key on a typewriter.

It is especially bothersome to punch a wrong key with an unforgiving computer system. *Forgiving systems* tolerate user errors, giving the person assistance in correcting the mistake. Unforgiving systems shut off, destroy data already entered, or otherwise punish the user when an error is detected. In what is perhaps the ultimate unforgiving system, a particular hardware and software combination produces the following output on the VDT screen when certain wrong keys are pressed: FATAL ERROR. Not surprisingly, many workers back off from the VDT quickly when that message appears.

Wise end-users will retreat permanently, avoiding such unfriendly systems even when the terminals are available only to experienced staff who are unlikely to commit errors. Because VDTs provide primary access to the computer system in most situations, selection of proper terminals is crucial. And as in other areas of the DP marketplace, the broad array of VDTs that are available makes proper selection easier. The right terminals help maintain organizational health. Selection of the wrong terminals might indeed be a fatal error.

Chapter 5

Making Decisions on the Right Bases

Decision makers often complain that they are not getting from the computer system the right kinds of information at the right times in the right formats. They find the information to be too detailed or to be about the wrong subject to help them in decision making. Especially irritating is being told by the DPers that the information is inside the computer memory but cannot economically be retrieved in the way the decision maker wants. "Why can't I get to the information if it's in there?" they ask.

One way to reduce these complaints is to take more responsibility for choosing how best to store the information inside computer memory. Putting those choices into action involves technical expertise usually possessed only by professional DPers. Still, by acquainting yourself with the alternatives and their costs and benefits, you are able to work along with the DPers to develop the most effective information storage and retrieval systems.

The information stored inside computer memory in a form ready for analysis is called the *data base*. Usually the data base is a pool of information. Various people throughout the organization contribute to it and each user in turn can call upon it. In sharing information in this way, users get the most from what is available. This sharing also can lead to more coordinated, unified actions in the organization and can enhance feelings of teamwork.

Almost always, there are a variety of data bases in the organization rather than just one big data base. This is true for a couple of reasons. First, different parts of the organization have different information needs. The Sales Department is interested in the market performance of competitors, but the Personnel Department is not. Personnel needs to know, for government reporting requirements, the ages and handicapped status of employees, but Sales does its best not to pay attention to such considerations. The content of data bases often overlaps. Both Personnel and Sales want to retrieve the figures telling the amounts of money sales staff earned in bonuses. Still, much of the information does not overlap, and it is too expensive to keep every sort of information in a form where it can be obtained quickly by every sort of department in the organization.

The expense is especially high if someone's privacy is violated, and that is the second reason for separate data bases. In a social service agency, Child Protective Services may maintain comprehensive records inside computer memory regarding abused children. Good clinical practice, if not the law, requires that welfare eligibility workers not be able to access the information. Sometimes the separation is a physical one. Confidential data are kept on a completely separate computer system. More frequently, confidential data are kept in the same computer system with less sensitive data, and access codes, such as passwords, are established so that only certain staff can access the confidential data.

When DPers talk about the data base, then, there is the implication of a number of data bases with each one being a pool of organizational knowledge. There also is the implication that the knowledge is stored in some organized way. In most computer systems, the organization is done with the assistance of *data base management systems*. These software tools improve efficiency by storing information in less space than it would otherwise consume inside computer memory and by retrieving information more quickly than would otherwise occur.

Data base management has its own set of words and terms. As in other areas of automation, the terminology can scare off a non-DPer. Yet overcoming any fright is important, for familiarity with the concepts represented by the words and terms helps you get the most from information available to you.

Some of the words and terms are illustrated in Figure 5.1, which is part of a personnel file. A *data item* is a unit of information. In Figure 5.1, the Employee Number for Steven Lewis is the example of a data item. But any of the items below the column headings could be considered a data item. The Department Number for Larry Jones is a data item, as is the entry French under Non-English Spoken for employee Cheryl Martin. A particular employee's salary level, the quantity ordered of a particular item, and the telephone number of a particular vendor would each be a data item in a data base that keeps those sorts of information.

An *entity* is a data item about which related data items are stored. In Figure 5.1, the example of an entity is Cheryl Martin because in the data base related data items, such as her Employee Number and Department Number, are kept regarding Ms. Martin. Each of the other names in the file is also an entity.

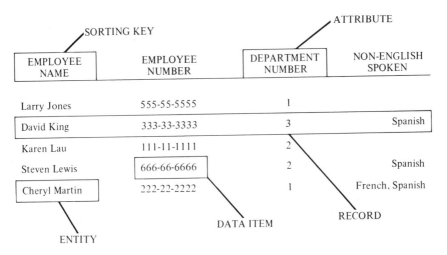

Figure 5.1 Data base management terminology.

An entity along with its related data items is called a *record*. For the record shown as an example in Figure 5.1, the entity is David King.

The column headings in Figure 5.1 are the *attributes*. An attribute is the type of information stored in the records. Department Number is the example, but Name, Employee Number, and Non-English Spoken are also attributes.

In what sounds like a circular definition, a *file* is defined as a group of records with common attributes. When the same kinds of information—attributes—are kept for a set of names or other entities, a file has been created. For this reason, Figure 5.1 might very well qualify as a file.

However, it might not qualify, for there is another condition in the definition of a file. It is not necessary that there be an entry of a data item for every combination of entity and attribute. However, it is necessary that the absence of an entry itself have a specific meaning.

Here is what that all translates to. In Figure 5.1, notice that for the entity Larry Jones there is a blank space under the attribute Non-English Spoken. If this is to be considered a file, the blank space must itself have a specific meaning. The most likely meaning is that, at least for public knowledge, Larry Jones speaks no languages other than English. If the blank space might mean this, or might mean that the information under the attribute hasn't been collected yet, or might mean something else entirely, then Figure 5.1 does not meet the formal definition of being a file.

The *sorting key* is the attribute used to put the records in order for output. In the example, the sorting key is Employee Name, since the order of the records is determined by the alphabetical order of the names of the employees. Records can be sorted in ascending order—from lowest to

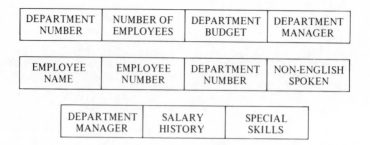

Figure 5.2   Attribute names for three simple files

highest—or in descending order—from highest to lowest, and there can be major sorting keys and minor sorting keys. For instance, you might want employee records listed by department name alphabetically, in ascending order, and within each department name listing, you might want the records to appear by employee salary starting with the highest salary and proceeding in descending order. In this case, your major sorting key is Department Name and your minor key is Employee Salary. Available data base management systems, more commonly called DBMS, allow many levels of sorting. You might sort accounts receivable records by client number, within that by delivery date, within that by order date, and within that by part number.

This brings up one important human factors issue in data base management. Don't bury yourself in details. Most people operate best with summarized data. They fail to detect the patterns and the exceptions as well when the output is cut up into a great number of categories. When a DBMS is first installed, it can be like a new toy. But don't be surprised when you later find yourself not wanting to use all of the capabilities. This is another instance of the general rule that you shouldn't exploit a system feature just because it is available.

The basis of order in output is the sorting key, or the set of sorting keys. The basis of organization of information inside computer memory is often attribute names that occur in different files. When various files have some attribute names in common, the collection is a data base.

An an illustration, consider Figure 5.2. Listed there are three files, or more accurately, the attribute names—the column headings—for three files. The middle file corresponds to the Employee File in Figure 5.1. The upper file is a Department File. Each record in the Department File will have a data item for Department Name, Number of Employees in that Department, Department Budget, and Department Manager's Name.

The third file listed contains three attribute names. In this file, there will be one record for each manager within the organization. This record will contain data items for the manager's name, the salary history of that manager, and special skills possessed by that manager.

This might be seen as a Managerial Skills Inventory. An organization is engaged in strategic planning, deciding where the organization is moving and what skills will be required among the managers for the organization to achieve its potential in the future. The Managerial Skills Inventory allows the organization to see the number of managers having the required skills and see where in the organization they are placed at present.

If inside computer memory is stored all of the records of the three files in Figure 5.2, this collection could be considered a data base. The organizing principle is the common attribute names between the files. The first and second files have the attribute Department Number, and the first and third have the attribute Department Manager. This is a relatively simple data base. In most cases, there will be a large number of different files with many instances in which the same attribute name occurs in a number of files.

DBMS differ in the ease with which information can be retrieved from various files and can be formatted in new ways. Often, information from one file can be accessed by going through another file. With one type of DBMS, called a hierarchical DBMS, records are said to own other records or to have parent–child relationships. It might be a one-to-many relationship. Each record in the Department File of Figure 5.2 might own many records in the Employee File—the records for employees in that department. It might be a one-to-one relationship. Each record in the Department File might own one record in the Managerial Skills Inventory—the record for the manager of that department.

Suppose that, using such a data structure and DBMS, you wanted to know special skills possessed by manager Carol Crawford. You could use just the third file to answer this question, entering the name and requesting as output the data items under the attribute Special Skills. You could also ask the question by Department Number, since Department File records own Managerial Skills Inventory records. So, entering the data base at the top file, you could ask, "What are the special skills of the manager of the Advertising Department?"

The problem with the hierarchical DBMS is that you can't easily go from a child record to a parent record. In the example, you could not easily receive an answer to the query, "What departments have managers with accounting skills?" This involves going from an attribute in a child file, the Managerial Skills Inventory, to an attribute in the parent file, the Department File.

Perhaps you will be told one day by your DPer, "I realize you've been collecting that information for two years now and that your staff have been taking the time to put it into the system. But even though all the information is in there, I just can't get it out to you in the form you want." As soon as your perfectly justified outrage cools, consider that what your DPer may be saying is that you are asking to navigate in the data base from a child to a parent record, and the DBMS can't do that efficiently.

One way to avoid this kind of situation is to create files with sufficient numbers of attributes. In the case of the Managerial Skills Inventory, you

DEPARTMENT MANAGER	DEPARTMENT NUMBER	SALARY HISTORY	SPECIAL SKILLS

Figure 5.3   Managerial Skills Inventory with four attributes.

could make an entry for each manager's Department Number. The file attributes would then look like Figure 5.3. When you wanted to know what departments have managers with accounting skills, you can have the system address just the file in Figure 5.3.

The price you pay with such a solution is repetition. Keeping a data item for Department Number in all three files increases the amount of storage space, and it costs money to store information inside computer memory. One advantage of a DBMS is that it lets you reduce redundancy by hooking together information in various files. The DBMS depends upon some duplication of attributes among the files to form the necessary connections. The common attribute names in the first and second files of Figure 5.2 and the first and third files in that figure allow the DBMS to move from one to the other. But when you intentionally go beyond the minimum to have many duplicate attributes or file segments, you surrender some of the advantages offered by a DBMS.

Redundancy also makes it harder to maintain data base accuracy. If you have three copies of Employee Address in the data base instead of one, you have much more than tripled the chance of making a mistake in updating. When it comes time to change an entry under Employee Address because an employee bought a new house, got married, or simply moved, someone is likely to forget to update that third copy.

A second type of DBMS is called the network DBMS. It is sometimes called a CODASYL DBMS because the Congress on Data Systems Languages developed the specifications for the network type. This kind of DBMS deals with the child-to-parent problem by having you anticipate the kinds of questions you'll be asking of the data base and then having the DPers set up a system of connections among the attributes. This system of connections, called a schema, allows the DBMS to navigate from one attribute to another, even if this means going from a child to a parent file.

With a network DBMS, it is important that you predict as well as you can the kinds of questions you'll be asking, for a change in the schema is often a major project. A third type of DBMS, called the relational, doesn't require you to predict your needs to such a great degree. With relational DBMS, you are pretty much free to inquire about relationships among any attributes in any files.

Relational DBMS accomplish this by setting up connections among the data item values themselves. These connections take up memory space that in some cases exceeds the memory space saved by the elimination of repetitive attributes.

Some DBMS allow both hierarchical and relational functions. With these dual capabilities, if an organization can anticipate well what queries will be made of the data base, the simpler hierarchical organization can be employed, and if there are likely to be changes in the types of questions posed to the data base and in the types of information kept, the more flexible relational organization can be employed.

Even with the relational DBMS, your questions are answered much more efficiently if those setting up the data base and choosing the DBMS expected you to ask those sorts of questions. It is therefore in your interest to tell DPers the *access keys* you plan to use. Access keys are the attributes, the column headings, in the files that form the basis of your questions. In the query, "What managers have accounting skills?," Special Skills is the access key. The DBMS will enter the data base looking for all instances in which Accounting occurs under the heading Special Skills and will then print out the matching Manager's Name for each of the identified records. In the query, "Print Department Number in which Number of Employees exceeds 100," the access key is Number of Employees.

Take special care to spot what might be called combination access keys. For instance, suppose you are likely to ask questions of the sort, "Which employees in Department 21 can speak Spanish?" Your access key is really two attributes—Department Number and Non-English Spoken.

Combination keys can be less obvious. Consider the query, "Print the price charged by Jones Plumbing for a sink." Here the access keys are Vendor Name and Item Name. Consider the query, "Print Department Numbers in which average annual employee salary exceeds $20,000." To answer this question, the DBMS will first sort out records by department number and will then calculate the average salary for each department number. The access keys are then Department Number and Employee Salary.

Because unexpected combination key queries frequently interfere with the efficient operation of the DBMS, be as complete as possible in predicting the kinds of questions you'll be asking the computer. This completeness in predictions also helps you judge what kinds of information to keep. If very few of the data base queries have to do with Non-English Spoken, why not use memory space to store something else instead? In addition to that, why spend money collecting the information in the first place if it isn't going to be used?

On the other hand, if there is a type of information you plan to use in the future, your predictions will signal you to begin collecting that information and signal the DPers to include it in the data base in a form you'll find to be valuable. A rule of thumb is that it takes one year to accumulate enough information to provide reliable averages when the computer performs its number crunching. Certainly such a rule is oversimplified, since there are cases where you could collect sufficient amounts of information in one day and other cases where you would have to keep records for decades to get enough data. Still, the rule of thumb does indicate the importance of anticipating information needs.

If those aren't sufficient reasons, there also is the point that planning increases the chances your data base will be used properly. If managers stop to think about their information needs, they are more likely to consult the information when it becomes available.

An organization called URBIS, for Urban Information Systems, suspected that municipalities were not using their available information to best advantage. In partnership with the Public Policy Research Organization, they evaluated ways in which data bases were being employed by a number of city governments that had installed computers. Ideally, when a city councilman or police chief wants to make a decision, the computer system is consulted, the output is digested by the councilman or police chief, and well-data-based conclusions are drawn. The researchers, found, however, that it was more common for the city official to make the decision first and then go to the computer system seeking out evidence to support the decision. Computer output was being consulted too late in the process. Answers were being confused with questions.

One explanation for the findings of the study is that the elected and appointed city officials didn't know what was in the data base and how to easily use it. If these city governments were like many other organizations, DPers set up the data base without adequately consulting the end-users.

Certainly some of the blame in these situations rests with the DPers. They can believe that, because design of the data base and selection of the DBMS involves technical factors, end-user input isn't relevant. Then too, DPers are under time pressures to produce results, and it is quicker to go ahead and do the work without continuing to consult the non-DP managers.

Much of the blame, however, rests with the end-users themselves who fail to get involved in data base planning, leaving these vital considerations to the DPers by default. The end-user's excuse might be that such planning takes too long, especially if it involves meeting repeatedly with the DPers as organizational demands change. Or the excuse might be that computers are intimidating and DPers hard to work with. But data base planning is too important for the non-DPers in your organization to avoid continuing involvement. Whatever the excuses of the DPers and the end-users, those excuses simply aren't good enough.

Chapter 6

Avoiding GIGO

As an end-user, you can control garbage coming out of the system by minimizing the amount of garbage that goes into the system. Take care in how information enters the computer. Two important aspects of this concern the design of forms for the collection of information and the design of procedures for assigning numbers to factors that will be entered into the system.

Remember that there are factors important in decision making that cannot legitimately have numbers assigned. These include matters like organizational politics and corporate social responsibility. In other cases, the factors come with numbers assigned, and it's just a matter of recording the numbers. You tell how good sales are by considering the number of units sold, or you judge the amount of driving that staff is doing by counting up the miles.

But, even with the pure numbers, you find yourself making adjustments. Maybe sales are traditionally higher in the summer months than in the winter months. You might apply a correction that takes account of these seasonal differences—multiplying winter month sales by 1.2 if summer month sales are traditionally 20 percent higher. Running averages are another sort of adjustment. Here, rather than looking at each month's figures alone, you might look at the average for months 1, 2, and 3; then the average for months 2, 3, and 4; then the average for months 3, 4, and 5; and so on. In this way, variations that are beyond your control have less effect on the numbers.

Make these adjustments with care to be sure they reflect what you intend. Once you start using seasonal corrections or running averages, you change the data, and it is as easy to distort the information as to bring it closer to reality. Wanting the data to come out in certain ways can readily lead you to make it come out in those ways.

After Ronald Reagan was elected President, David A. Stockman used the computers of the Office of Management and Budget to analyze economic statistics. At first, the output did not support the supply-side policies of the Reagan administration. What was Stockman's reaction? He changed the way the data were analyzed, both by altering parameters in the computer software and by having a group of staff further analyze the data after they came out of the computer.

There are those who say Stockman was dishonest because he was changing the data to fit his preconceived notions. Others say Stockman was correctly searching for other interpretations of the data. In any case, it is clear that the Reagan administration policies affected the steps Stockman took. It is another example of the importance in not placing an exactness on something because it is associated with numbers. The way the economic statistics come out depends to a fair extent upon who is doing the calculating.

If you're using the figures to convince a colleague or customer of a specific point, creative manipulation may be in your best interest. But if you're trying to get an objective look at a situation before making up your mind on a course of action, reduce the effects of any biases on the computer analyses. Current software packages allow you to make a great many adjustments to the information. While using these capabilities, be asking yourself how you want the analyses to come out and judge the extent to which your desires are distorting your methodology.

Dealing with numbers such as sales figures and economic statistics challenges you to come up with honest adjustments. Dealing with factors like organizational politics challenges you to acknowledge that some important information can't be legitimately quantified, and if this information resides within computer memory, it is best handled as words rather than as numbers. The challenge with some other qualitative factors is to transform them into numbers in the right ways.

As an example, consider customer satisfaction. It's nice to be able to assign a number to the degree of satisfaction of each customer, for in this way the computer can number crunch to determine average satisfaction for various groups and under various circumstances.

Figure 6.1 presents a scale used by an organization to determine the degree of customer satisfaction. Each customer surveyed was presented the four choices in Figure 6.1 and asked to mark the choice that best represented his or her degree of satisfaction. The numbers along the sides of Figure 6.1 were not presented to the customer. As described below, these scales were used to translate the customer responses into numbers to be entered into the computer.

Figure 6.1 illustrates two points regarding the quantification of qualitative factors. First, notice that there is no neutral category. On this scale, you are

Please place a checkmark next to the item that comes closest to indicating how satisfied you are with our services:

First-glance scoring scheme				Selected scoring scheme
1	( )	Highly dissatisfied		2
2	( )	Somewhat dissatisfied		2
3	( )	Somewhat satisfied		4
4	( )	Highly satisfied		5

Figure 6.1. Scale for surveying and quantifying customer satisfaction.

either satisfied or dissatisfied, nothing in-between. Few people in this world are completely neutral about anything. However, when you give people a middle category, they will select it. Given a neutral category, if the customers are dissatisfied, they often say, "Neither satisfied nor dissatisfied," because they are kind. If they are dissatisfied, they often select the middle category because they don't like to commit themselves.

When many people select the neutral category, it doesn't tell you much. It has few implications for action, and so it isn't truly information. By eliminating the middle category, you force respondents to make a choice, and this gives you more useful findings.

Like many of the suggestions in this book, there are qualifications and exceptions. For one thing, if you are asking people who they will vote for in the next election, a neutral category, such as "None of the above," does give you useful information. In any sort of survey, encourage respondents to make comments. Although you often can't easily translate these into numbers, the comments can suggest categories and alternatives for future surveys.

An experience of the United States military provides an example of an exception to the rule of avoiding the neutral category. The U.S. Army studies the attitudes of troops toward weapons systems by asking them to use a scale like that in Figure 6.1 with the addition of a middle, neutral category. The middle one was added after U.S. Army research concerning questionnaire design. This research found that when there is no neutral category, soldiers who would have selected that neutral one switch to the dissatisfied side more often than they switch to the satisfied side. It is as if the soldiers are accustomed to complaining, and those deprived of a chance to say they don't care one way or the other would rather complain than praise.

Yet the military doesn't want to spend funds trying to improve a system that the troops can tolerate, even if they aren't enthusiastic about the system. This, then, is one case where a large number of neutral answers does have implications for action. The action consists of spending resources on improving systems other than the ones judged neither satisfying nor dissatisfying.

There is a second point illustrated by Figure 6.1. Do not automatically use the scoring scheme that first comes to mind. The scheme that first comes to mind for managers is listed in the column on the far left of Figure 6.1. Here, if a customer reports high dissatisfaction, a 1 is entered into the computer for averaging, and if the report is, "Somewhat satisfied," a 3 is entered. The scoring scheme selected is listed along the right-hand side of Figure 6.1. With this scheme, "Highly dissatisfied" is equivalent to a 2, and "Somewhat satisfied" is equivalent to a 4. The reason this scheme was selected has to do with findings from marketing research conducted by the company.

Said the company, "We will use the same rating equivalent for 'Highly dissatisfied' and 'Somewhat dissatisfied' because our marketing research indicates a customer is equally unlikely to use our services in the future if one of those two alternatives is selected. Beyond a certain base rate, we are willing to expend twice as much in the way of resources to move a customer from a dissatisfied category to the 'Somewhat satisfied' category. Therefore, the numerical equivalent for 'Somewhat satisfied' will be 2×2, or 4. We are willing to expend about 25 percent more to move the person to the 'Highly satisfied' category. This is because our marketing research suggests that if a person reports being somewhat satisfied, that person is likely to use our services again, but people who report high satisfaction will, in addition, recommend us to a business associate, and that is the major source of new business we've targeted."

The company was creating a scoring scheme that reflected, in the relationships among the numbers, the intended assumptions. Do the same with the scales that you create.

Proper questionnaire construction isn't easy. Even things like the order of the alternatives can have an influence. Suppose, for instance, that the order of choices on the satisfaction scale were reversed, with "Highly satisfied" coming first and "Highly dissatisfied" coming last. It is likely that the pattern of answers among the choices would change as well, for some people select the first choice on a question regardless of whether that first choice indicates satisfaction or indicates dissatisfaction. Try out various ways of phrasing your questions and try out various orders of the alternatives to find out, over time, what provides you the most useful results. The memory and processing speed of the computer allow you to quickly analyze the various findings and relate them to other factors. These factors include the ways the questions are presented, and they also include the region in which the questions were asked, how long after product or service delivery the survey was done, and even the time of day of the responses.

The design of the form itself should reflect the logic of the information being collected. If monthly figures over a one-year period are to be entered, then the 12 blank lines should be in a column, one over the other. If the name, address, birthdate, and case number of every client are to be entered, each type of information should begin on a new line or have its own distinctive space on the form.

Why is the item being returned?

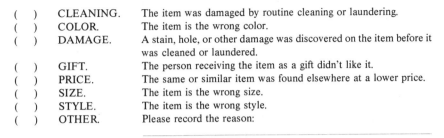

( ) CLEANING.   The item was damaged by routine cleaning or laundering.
( ) COLOR.   The item is the wrong color.
( ) DAMAGE.   A stain, hole, or other damage was discovered on the item before it
                        was cleaned or laundered.
( ) GIFT.   The person receiving the item as a gift didn't like it.
( ) PRICE.   The same or similar item was found elsewhere at a lower price.
( ) SIZE.   The item is the wrong size.
( ) STYLE.   The item is the wrong style.
( ) OTHER.   Please record the reason:

Figure 6.2. Source document section for indicating why clothing was returned, with alternatives in alphabetical order

Sometimes there is more than one logical way to structure the form. Imagine that you direct a chain of retail clothing stores and you've noticed that the number of returned items has increased recently. Intending to take corrective action, you want to collect information about why items are being returned. From talking with a group of salesclerks, you learn that the most common single reason given by customers for returns is that the size is wrong, and that other common reasons include the item being an undesired gift, the item reacting poorly to being cleaned or laundered, and the customer finding the same or similar item elsewhere at a lower price.

You might design a source document that includes the scale in Figure 6.2. With this form, the salesperson can place a mark in a box rather than needing to write in the reason. This saves time for the salesperson. However, does Figure 6.2 illustrate the best order of the alternatives? The alternatives are in alphabetical order by a key word for the reason. If a customer returns an items and says the size is wrong, the salesclerk looks for "Size" in alphabetical order.

But you have learned from your interviews that the most common single reason given for a return is that the item is the wrong size. Perhaps it would be better to put "Size" first on the list and have the other alternatives listed in order of how frequently they come up. The list might look like Figure 6.3. In this way, the salesclerk is usually marking a box toward the top of the form, and this saves at least a little more time.

These are some problems with the arrangement in Figure 6.3. Your interviews told you only that size was the most frequently given reason. The differences in frequency among the other alternatives may not be significant. It might actually take longer for the salesclerk to find the right category, especially if it isn't "Size," than if the alternatives were in alphabetical order.

A more important problem with the Figure 6.3 format, as well as with placing the choices in alphabetical order, is that these arrangements don't reflect well the way in which the information is probably going to be

Why is this item being returned?

( )   SIZE.   The item is the wrong size.
( )   GIFT.   The person receiving the item as a gift didn't like it.
( )   CLEANING.   The item was damaged by routine cleaning or laundering.
( )   PRICE.   The same or similar item was found elsewhere at a lower price.
( )   COLOR.   The item is the wrong color.
( )   DAMAGE.   A stain, hole, or other damage was discovered on the item before it
                       was cleaned or laundered.
( )   STYLE.   The item is the wrong style.
( )   OTHER.   Please record the reason:

Figure 6.3.   Clothing return question with alternatives approximately in order of frequency of
response

presented by the customer. The most important logic to consider in forms design is the logic of how information will be presented for recording on the form. Consider this dialogue between customer and salesclerk.

"I want to return this blouse. The receipt is in the bag."
"May I ask why you're returning it."
"I gave it as a gift, and the person I gave it to didn't like it."
"All right. I'll mark 'Gift' on the form here."
"She said it was the wrong size."
"I guess I should mark 'Size,' too."
"But I think the real reason she told me to take it back is that she doesn't like my taste in style. She didn't want to hurt my feelings, so she said it was because of the size."

At about this point, the salesclerk is ready to hand the form to the customer and say, "Here. You fill it out yourself." And that might not be such a bad idea. By asking the customer to fill out the form, you remove one step in the analysis of the information—the translation by the salesclerk of what the customer is saying. The less the distance between the data and the CPU, the greater the accuracy of the output. Asking the customer to record the information is still another time-saving measure for the salesclerk, although it is important for the salesclerk to look over the completed form and confirm that the customer understood what was to be done.

When the customer fills out the form, it also increases the chances that the genuine reasons will be revealed. Customers might feel uncomfortable telling the clerk aloud and directly that they can get a better price on the item elsewhere, but those customers might be quite willing to mark it on a form. If customers are finding better prices elsewhere, this is important to know. You could lower your own prices or advertise value points like your broad selection and extremely liberal return policy.

Figure 6.4 illustrates a format that takes account of the ways the person returning the clothing is probably thinking. The form makes it clear that more than one alternative can be marked. Notice also that the alternative most likely to be checked is near the last. The reason is that, in spite of the instructions to mark as many choices as apply, the customer becomes less likely to go on as more alternatives are marked. If "It's the wrong size" masks the true reason, the true reason is more likely to be indicated when "Size" comes after that reason on the form.

"Size" is not the very last choice because the last specific choice, "Gift," is a "none of the above" type of category. Knowing that the recipient didn't like the item of clothing doesn't tell you why the person didn't like it. It is useful to know that the item was a gift. The implication for action, if that category is marked frequently, might be to advertise gift certificates more aggressively. Collecting the additional information about why the gift wasn't acceptable has implications for action as well.

Still, don't try to collect too much information. People don't like to fill out long questionnaires. Avoid GIGO by keeping forms short. It might be nice to know, for instance, whether the person returning the gift is the one who bought the gift, the one who received the gift, or somebody else entirely. Or it could help to know the color of a returned item if the color is considered wrong so that merchandise won't be ordered in clearly undesired hues. But longer questionnaires produce less accuracy and more upset from the respondents. Distinguish the material you need to know from what it would be nice to know.

Placing "Cleaning" before "Damage" in the Figure 6.4 format again reflects information processing order. Did the damage seem to be caused by cleaning? If "Damage" came first, the customer might mark that one, go on to "Cleaning," notice that alternative should have been marked, but then decide it's too much trouble to erase the mark already made, and so just leave the mark by "Damage."

Why is the item being returned? Please put an "X" next to all the reasons for the return.

( )	COLOR.	The item is the wrong color.
( )	STYLE.	The item is the wrong style.
( )	PRICE.	The same or similar item was found elsewhere at a lower price.
( )	CLEANING.	The item was damaged by routine cleaning or laundering.
( )	DAMAGE.	There is a stain, hole, or other damage on the item, and it doesn't look like it was caused by cleaning or laundering
( )	SIZE.	The item is the wrong size.
( )	GIFT.	The person receiving the item as a gift didn't like it.
( )	OTHER.	Please write down the reason:

/ /

Figure 6.4. Clothing return question with alternatives in an information processing order

Talk to the people who will be filling out the form. When the source document is an order form, talk with the people who take the orders to see what design ideas they have. When the source document is to be a record of problems in the manufacturing plant, ask the people working in the plant about the circumstances under which they'll be filling it out. Perhaps it will be completed next to a machine where there is poor lighting, so extra-large lettering is important. A cardboard backing on each form could be helpful if clipboards aren't readily available for plant floor personnel.

All of this seems distant from understanding how computer systems work. But the distance isn't so much when you consider that a crucial component of the well-functioning computer system is accurate information, and it is people who provide the information. With number crunching, garbage can be mixed in so well alongside useful data that you don't notice the garbage when you look at the averages. The best place to reduce erroneous output is at the input side. Source documents are as much a part of the computerized decision making system as are hardware and software.

Talk not only with the people who will record information on the form, but also with the people who will be reading the form. They, too, want simplicity in design. One example of simplicity is printing on the merchandise return form the most common responses rather than asking the salesclerk or customer to write down the reason in each case. It is easier to mark a box than to write down the words, and it is much easier to read the preprinted alternative next to a checkmark than to dicipher a handwritten phrase.

On almost any form, an "Other. Please State" category is necessary. With that sort of alternative, where the reply will be handwritten, have vertical lines dividing the horizontal response line, as is done in the last alternative in Figure 6.4. This keeps the respondent from running letters or numbers together in the reply. Another method for accomplishing this same goal is to use a line of boxes with instructions to place one letter or number in each box.

In designing the form so that people can more easily read it, you are also making it easier for a machine to read the form. Optical scanning devices that read checkmarks have been available for many years. There are also devices that read typewritten characters. Early versions could read only certain type styles, and these styles were not always legible to humans. Often, the equipment that entered the information onto the source document would type one version for optical scanning and, at the same time, print another version adjacent to it for human reading. Current optical scanning devices can read a wide variety of typewritten character fonts, including pica and elite.

Optical scanning is another way to reduce the distance between the data and the CPU, thereby increasing accuracy. Supermarkets that use these machines to read the Universal Product Codes from merchandise obtain more valid data than when a human store checker has to read the price and then push buttons on a cash register to enter the information. On items in the warehouse, attach tags with codes that can be optically scanned, and it becomes much easier to obtain an accurate record of the items being stored.

The cost of optical scanning devices is decreasing at the same time that the accuracy of these devices increases. Design your source documents so a machine can read them. With the optical scanners, data entry is quicker and more garbage free. Until the machines come, a form designed for optical scanning is probably easier for a person to read than one designed without these considerations in mind.

The vertical lines and the boxes for the "Other. Please State" alternatives are an example. Optical scanning devices to read handwritten entries do not have the same accuracy as those for typewritten materials, and they likely never will have that accuracy because of the variety with which people write and the casual quality of most handwriting. But in discouraging the respondent from running letters or numbers together, you do make it easier for a machine to read the material accurately as well as for a person to read it accurately.

You can combine the best of automated and manual data entry. With a form like that in Figure 6.4, if one of the preprinted choices is checked, the optical scanning device enters the response. If the "Other. Please write down the reason" choice is marked, the device can signal a human operator to read the handwritten information and type it in.

Another example of this combining is to have the information that is read in by an optical scanner then displayed on a screen where a human being can spot errors. The machine is better than the human in getting information in accurately, but the human is better than the machine in judging the seriousness of an input error when it does occur. Some organizations are using optical scanners, along with human editing, to very quickly enter the contents of printed court decisions into a data base used by attorneys.

That distance between the data and the CPU is reduced even further with screen data entry. Here an end-user types information directly into the CPU instead of entering the information onto a source document and then having another person key it in or having a device read the source document. The proliferation of data entry terminals throughout most organizations has made more screen data entry possible. As with the source document, the screen format should be as simple as possible and should reflect the logic of the information being entered.

When designing source documents or screen entry formats, collaboration with DPers is important. If the document is to be readable by a machine, someone familiar with machine capabilities should review the layout of the form. Similarly, there are system limitations on screen format design, although these limitations are not as great as many end-users come to believe. Screen generation software allows you to rearrange the structure of the screen format. Work with the DPers to devise layouts that seem right and then try them for a time. Be ready to revise. Don't tell the DPers you've firmly decided on a format until the people who actually have to carry out the input tasks have had ample opportunity to see how livable the format is. In the same way, don't have 200,000 copies of a source document printed up to start with. Print up a few hundred, try them out, make needed changes, review the changes with the DPers, and then print up some acceptable revised versions.

The key notion is collaboration. Design must not be a matter of what is easiest for the hardware and software without attention to what fits the characteristics of the data and is easiest for the users. Remember that information and people are two of the four components of the computerized decision making system. Just as the wrong kinds of information can go into the computer system for analysis, the wrong kinds of considerations can take over in system planning. Just as there can be garbage in system output, there can be garbage in system design.

Chapter 7

Feeling Secure

Not too much time goes by before we again come across a report in a newspaper or on the radio about somebody vandalizing or misusing a computer system. In fact, the United States Department of Commerce estimates that only 1 out of 100 instances of computer crime is ever discovered. This statistic must be considered with some suspicion. After all, if the crime was never discovered, how do you know it exists?

Still, those who work with computers feel comfortable in saying that the vast majority of computer crimes are not discovered. Much of the reason has to do with the nature of the workplace. Most shoplifting from retail stores and theft by employees from warehouses is never discovered either, for it would be prohibitively expensive to maintain surveillance sufficient to root out all crime using methods acceptable in a free society.

A significant difference between computer crime and other types is the amount of money involved. According to FBI statistics, the average gain from a computer-assisted bank embezzlement is about 150 times as much as the take from a traditional bank robbery. One important characteristic of computer crime to remember is that once the perpetrator begins, it is easier to continue the crime than to stop. A trapdoor is opened, the money or information flows through, and the chance of discovery is greater in slamming the trapdoor shut than in distracting attention while keeping the trapdoor open.

Because of the large losses involved, organizations have traditionally hesitated to report computer crimes. The fear is that the organization will look bad. The price of the stock will go down. Venture capital will be harder to raise. If there is a fiduciary relationship, as with a bank or an insurance company, the public won't want to trust the organization with money. If there is a consumer relationship, the consumers won't shop there any more because they'll think the prices are being raised artifically to compensate for the losses from computer crimes.

Many of these fears have little basis in fact. Actually, there are probably some companies that could benefit from the publicity that comes after reports of being victimized. But a better reason does exist for notifying law enforcement agencies when a computer crime is discovered. The notification can lead to investigations that make such crimes less likely to occur in the future. There are organizations that have devoted themselves to the study of computer misuse. You might decide that it is best to limit the publicity, or you might choose not to press for apprehension and prosecution of the offender. However, you are helping other organizations as well as your own when you report computer crimes.

The stories we do read about or hear about usually involve large sums of money. But computer crime can be just a plain bother for the organization's managers, even when the monetary loss is small. Computers at Sandia Labs in Albuquerque, New Mexico were being used in a bookmaking scheme. From one perspective, this is a fine application of data processing capabilities. You can use the number crunching to calculate odds and point spreads. Word processing would be useful in sending out notices to those in debt, telling them to pay up or else. Risk management software might be employed to predict the consequences if you don't honor your own debts to a particular individual. From an organizational perspective, however, this is no way to use an expensive, powerful computer system.

An early reaction of senior managers at Sandia Labs was to order a check of the other contents of computer memory. They figured that if bookmaking data were in there, other mischief might also be in there. They found a good amount of it: Recipes, jokes, video game instructions, rosters of the Sandia Labs bowling teams. One employee was even storing a catalog of a beer bottle collection.

The next reaction of senior management was to order that the extraneous material be removed. Because Sandia Labs conducts highly sensitive government research regarding nuclear energy, the United States Department of Energy asked Sandia Labs management to check back some time later. Management, to their chagrin, found that extraneous material was still there.

Another characteristic of computer crime is that the perpetrators often look upon it as some kind of video game. They see themselves as dealing with electronic impulses, not really money. They see themselves as matching wits with a machine, not as stealing from their employer. The computer has democratized crime. So many of us now have access to the system that so many of us can vandalize or misuse the system, and we fail to see it as even a petty criminal act.

Still, it is at least a petty crime, and even petty crime is a nuisance. Perhaps the best illustration is provided by an incident that occurred at a Washington, D.C. office of the Internal Revenue Service. Some employees there were using the computer system to credit themselves with unearned vacation hours and sick leave hours. When senior management discovered the ruse, they summarily removed the offending employees from their workstations. It was not too long afterward that those senior managers came to realize what they had chased out the door was the entire knowledge of the automated payroll system. They couldn't make out the paychecks. The IRS had to bring those employees back, process the payroll, train new staff, and then once again terminate the offenders. What a nuisance for the organization!

One approach to reducing computer crime is to screen employees carefully before allowing them access to the computers. Because of the chronic shortages of qualified DPers, a number of organizations have inadvertently hired criminals. A university hired, as a data center manager, a man who had previously been convicted of embezzlement. The administrators of that university would certainly have been surprised had they completed a thorough background investigation. However, the administrators received their big surprise anyway when they learned that their employee was committing his favorite crime on the university computers. To add to that, those administrators also discovered that another member of the data center staff also had a criminal record.

Employee screening is more difficult because of *distributed data processing* (DDP). DDP means giving increased responsibility to end-users for input, processing, and storage concerns in addition to their use of the output. The rallying cry of DDP is, "A computer terminal on every employee's desk," Where every employee has direct access to the computers, employee screening can mean doing a background check on everybody. But most organizations, aside from those doing high-level security work don't want to spend funds to thoroughly research the history of each computer user. In addition, there are skilled, completely honest employees who would vigorously object to such thorough research.

Some compromises should be made. Do complete background checks only on those employees who will have open access to the computer system. Then control access in a DDP organization based upon what each employee legitimately needs to know to competently carry out his or her job functions.

An approach to screening with more pitfalls than background checks is personality testing. The argument is that certain sorts of people are especially likely to commit computer crimes, and there are tests that can identify those people. Both parts of the argument lack validity. As to the second part, personality tests are simply not accurate enough to identify any kind of trait with the exactness you'd require to grant or deny employment to a person.

Ability or skills testing can be useful in selecting DPers, for there is an association between performance on a test of clerical aptitude and performance on the job as a computer programmer. But no such match exists for tests of honesty and related personality characteristics.

As to the first part of the argument—certain types of people are especially likely to commit computer crimes—in reality there are many kinds of motivations. There are computer criminals who don't understand the machines well, but are fascinated by computer capabilities and see computers as tools for thievery. There are others who pride themselves on a technical knowledge of data processing and on their ability to outwit the security safeguards, even if the monetary gain is small. There are those who hate the machines and will stick foreign objects into disk drives, feed erroneous instructions into the CPU, or shoot bullets into the VDT.

The tendency to commit a computer crime comes from a combination of the personality characteristics of the perpetrator and the characteristics of the situation. If you focus on the personality characteristics of the users, you can stop people from using the computers when they should be using them. You will find yourself confusing assertiveness with aggression or confusing creativity with deviousness in managers you evaluate. Beyond that, if you deny someone full employment opportunities because of a personality evaluation, you'll soon find yourself being summoned before a judge. Focus instead on the characteristics of situations that lead to computer misuse and vandalism.

There is, for example, evidence that computer crime is more likely when employees feel they are not being paid fairly. Actually, it may be that most of us feel we are not being paid fairly, but the greater the amount of perceived unfairness, the greater the temptation. Good salary administration, then, helps curb computer crime.

In addition, an open-door policy for handling employee grievances is important. It should not be necessary for an employee to kick the organization in the shins by misusing the computers if that employee feels he or she is being treated unfairly. An employee shouldn't be tempted to sell your organization's software or time on the organization's computers to outsiders to earn money that compensates for what the employee sees as an insufficient salary. When your subordinates know they can freely talk out grievances with you, they are less interested in exploiting the computer system to get your attention.

There also is evidence that computer crime is more likely when employees feel little intellectual challenge in their work. Unfortunately, office automation has frequently pressured human beings into acting like robots. Managers forget that people think differently and act differently from machines. Sometimes the computers were acquired with the argument that they will allow the organization to operate using fewer employees. When the machines arrive, the users are then expected to produce at superhuman rates. It takes time to learn how to use the equipment well, and computers can be at their best in reducing the amount of paper produced, not increasing the amount.

Among bright employees, the high pressure produces two results. First, these people will come to dislike the computer system and the organization. Second, these people will notice that the intellectual challenge is gone from their daily work. The two results will, in turn, motivate users to reintroduce the challenge and release some hostility by playing computer games where the organization's resources and security measures are the target.

Computers provide great opportunities for improving the quality of work life. Boring operational control decisions can be delegated to the computer, freeing time for the more interesting activities like strategic planning and implementation of decisions through direct work with people. In the long term, computers help organizations make money and save money. But the pressures to manage by the numbers alone or to effect immediate cost savings can create a high-pressure, boring workplace in which computer mischief thrives.

When introducing computers, expect the costs to rise in the short term over the cost of the manual procedures. There will be the additional expenses of system acquisition and for the planning that came before system acquisition. There also will be the additional expenses in employee retraining and in keeping both the manual and automated systems going until you are confident of the automated system's reliability. Do not place yourself in the position of having to turn people into automatons because you've promised to save money immediately.

An overly permissive office environment also can encourage computer crime. Many managers figure that people will make copies of sheet music on the photocopy machine and steal paper clips to replenish the supply at home, and that the costs in time and good will would be excessive if such transgressions were to be stamped out. This attitude can slip over into one of tolerating employee use of the phones for lengthy personal calls across the country and then perhaps pilferage of small office equipment. It would, in fact, be prohibitively expensive to discover all instances of employee theft, let alone eliminate them. Still, the effort should be made to control employee misuse and misappropriation of the organization's resources. If these petty crimes are freely tolerated, employees can interpret that tolerance as license to test the limits even further.

The particular problem with misuse and misappropriation of the computers is that the costs climb so fast. One aspect of this is the trapdoor dilemma: When an employee starts misusing the computers, it is easier to continue than to chance discovery by stopping. The losses from computer crime then grow much faster than those from stealing paper clips or making personal telephone calls. Another aspect is that the release of some of the information inside the computer system can greatly hurt an organization. If an angry employee sells to a competing business the mailing list of your top customers or detailed budget figures or a secret manufacturing formula, the release of the information is only the start of the damage that will surely occur.

Again, decide who should have access to what information. Collaborate with the DPers in setting up *passwords* or access codes, which are words or numbers allowing different people to use the system in different ways. Sometimes each employee will have an individual password that identifies him or her to the system, and each manager knows the passwords of the employees he or she supervises. In other cases, passwords are shared by groups of employees and the manager has another password that acts like a master key, allowing access to what would otherwise require a group of passwords.

Who can read the contents of the data base, but not change the contents? Who can make changes? Who verifies that the changes have been made correctly? Who can delete information from the data base? Who decides who can and cannot do each of these? Such decisions should be made at a senior management level, and they can then be put into effect using a system of passwords.

Set clear policies as to what constitutes misuse of the computers. This helps employees monitor themselves and each other. It also allows managers to legitimately administer discipline if computer security has been breached. The policies should be realistic and should indicate that certain actions are more serious than others. Keeping software code confidential is very important if your organization has been granted a license for use of the software with a condition that the code not be revealed. Intentional damage of a system component is serious, with the degree of seriousness depending upon the amount of damage and value of the contents. Using the computer to balance a personal checking account is a relative misdemeanor.

The challenge in developing policies is to be specific enough so that the employees understand the code of conduct, but not so specific that you are providing detailed instructions about the various ways an employee can damage the computer system and the organization. It is always better to say what should be done than what should not be done. Actually, some organizations specifically sanction use of the computers by employees for personal purposes. "Now that Karl has his entire investment portfolio loaded into our computers, he'll think twice before quitting," said one executive about a valuable subordinate.

The trouble with this attitude is that Karl, as well as the executive, may not know the limits of what is being allowed. Is it all right if Karl uses computer time to evaluate various personal investment options? How about hooking up to the Dun and Bradstreet data bank for a daily rundown on stocks in his portfolio? There is a cogent argument for allowing staff to use the computer system for their own purposes as a perquisite of employment, and perks are more likely to be handled on an informal basis than in comprehensive written policies. Be as sure as possible that there is at least a clear understanding of what is intended.

Another questionable use of business computers is for playing video games. As soon as a new arcade game appears in the pizza parlors, an adaptation begins its journey toward business computers worldwide. In an effort to make software packages more user friendly, some vendors introduce the packages in the context of a video game.

Look for packages that don't depend upon being cute for their appeal to users. Software packages in an organization must serve a serious business purpose. A playful attitude on the job can certainly add to creativity. Business simulation games help managers learn without risking real corporate money. But the arcade games create an attitude surrounding the computers that is playful in the wrong way.

Check not only your own end-user policies, but also the policies of data processing departments. If your DPers have written policies about computer misuse, that is in no way a guarantee they will abide by them. However, if there are no written policies, that is a virtual guarantee that protecting privacy, confidentiality, and security are not high priorities.

Maybe your organization deals with *service bureaus*, or time-sharing bureaus, which are organizations outside your own that use their computers to provide you data processing. This definition covers a broad range of endeavors. There are service bureaus that do contract programming. Others provide you VDTs and character printers on your premises and have the CPU, main memory, secondary memory, and other equipment at their site, with communication over telephone lines. There are also service bureaus that, for one lease price, provide you on your premises all the hardware, software, maintenance, consultation, and training you require.

In an industry so broad ranging, it is pleasantly surprising that there are not more instances of security breaches. Still, ask to see the service bureau's policies regarding computer misuse and protection of their clients' information. It is an advantage if employees of the service bureau are bonded. You might want to insist that the service bureau not do business with any organization that is a direct competitor of yours, although this can lead to you having to select a service bureau that is less desirable in other ways.

If yours is a critical application, communication over *dedicated* telephone lines might be indicated. In data processing, dedicated means reserved. Dedicated telephone lines are reserved for your use, where the regular telephone lines are used by whatever person or computer is making a phone call at that time. Dedicated telephone lines are harder to tap than public lines, so your information is more likely to be kept confidential. The balancing factor is that dedicated lines are more expensive, and you may not need the protection for all of your processed data.

Distributed data processing and the emergence of service bureaus have created certain security concerns. Another DP trend that affects security is integration of the system. In the integrated system, output from one task becomes input for another task. One piece of paper does more. Consider how an integrated system might operate in a company that makes custom

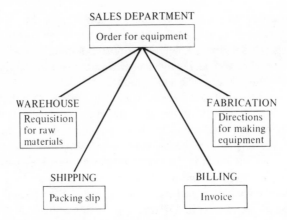

SALES DEPARTMENT

Order for equipment

WAREHOUSE

Requisition
for raw
materials

FABRICATION

Directions
for making
equipment

SHIPPING

Packing slip

BILLING

Invoice

Figure 7.1 Example of an integrated system.

equipment. The process begins with the receipt by the sales department of an order for equipment. This one piece of paper, the order form, triggers off a set of actions, as diagramed in Figure 7.1. As soon as the contents of the order form are entered into the computer system, the system uses information inside the data base to translate the order into manufacturing specifications. A list of the raw supplies needed is sent to the warehouse, and a list of directions for making the equipment is sent to the fabrication department. The computer system also automatically employs the order form contents to produce a packing slip to be used by the shipping department and the invoice to be used by the billing department.

There can be further degrees of integration. The requisition for raw materials can automatically debit the inventory record for that item kept inside the data base. When the inventory gets below a certain level, the system can automatically produce an order that is sent through purchasing to the supplier of the item.

In this example, it is likely that along the way paper will be produced. There will be printed requisitions to the warehouse, directions to the fabrication department, packing slips to shipping, invoices to billing, and order forms for purchasing. This paper creates an *audit trail*, and this is the important feature for computer security. An audit trail is output that can be read by a manager and can be used to trace back the cause of errors or computer misuse.

Suppose, for instance, that an enterprising billing clerk adds to each invoice a small charge for a modularity debugger and then pockets the additional amount when payment arrives. If the accounts receivable records are available on paper rather than just inside computer memory, and if a paper copy of the original packing slip can be compared with a paper copy of the original invoice, discovery of the misdeed is easier.

Audit trails often become less thorough as a system is integrated. One copy of the invoice is produced and sent to the customer. There is no paper copy stored by the organization, for it is felt that if one is needed, it can always be produced from the magnetic traces of the data base. A reorder might be sent out to a supplier of raw materials without a purchasing manager ever looking it over carefully.

To protect security, have a human being regularly review the products of the integrated computer system to spot signs of mischief. It costs money and takes time to have the computers produce additional paper all along the way and to have skilled people audit the system. However, the loss is far outweighed in importance by the gain in validity and reliability.

A method for improving security that is related to audit trails is backup copies. Have duplicates of the information, the software, and the user manuals available. Then, if the data base, the computer programs, or the manuals are altered, discovery of the alteration and corrections to the system are both easier. One backup method is called the *grandfather system*. The grandfather system involves making a duplicate copy of information and storing that duplicate copy some distance from the original.

Consider how the grandfather system might work in a university office that keeps records of student grades. This office has heard the reports of students gaining access to computerized student transcripts and altering grades, often simply as a prank directed against another student, but also often as a way of looking good without working hard. The office decides to have a backup copy of grades that can be compared with the original. Grades are submitted each academic quarter, and the updating of the transcripts is done on magnetic disks that hold the contents of all transcripts for current students. When the updating is completed, the contents of the disks are copied onto magnetic tapes, and these tapes are stored in a bank vault located across town from the library holding the disks.

In the grandfather system, the disk with the original copy on it is referred to as the son. The duplicate, on tape in this case, is called the father. The father replaces the tape that was stored the last time a copy was made. This former father is referred to as the grandfather. The grandfather is taken back to the data center and, in a twist that does not cleanly parallel real life, the grandfather is prepared to become a father again. That is, new data from a disk is copied onto the tape.

In the university office's application of the grandfather system, there is an additional step along the way before a new father is produced and the old father becomes a grandfather. This is illustrated in Figure 7.2. When the current versions of the transcripts are ready on the disks, the transcript for each student includes two parts. First, the transcript includes grades for courses just completed. Second, the transcript includes grades for courses taken in prior quarters. Since the grades for courses just completed are being entered into the system for the first time, the real worry about grade alterations concerns the past grades. University staff fear that, during an

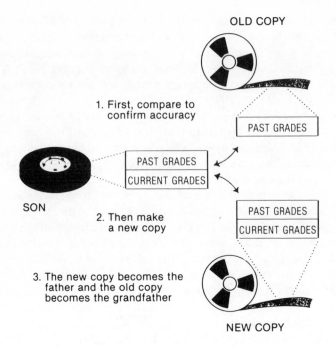

OLD COPY

1. First, compare to
   confirm accuracy

PAST GRADES

PAST GRADES

CURRENT GRADES

SON

2. Then make
   a new copy

PAST GRADES

CURRENT GRADES

3. The new copy becomes the
   father and the old copy
   becomes the grandfather

NEW COPY

Figure 7.2 Example of the grandfather system's use in security control.

academic term, students will gain access to the system and change grades from courses taken in prior academic quarters.

A student could make changes on the son, which is the version of the transcripts kept on magnetic disks in the university offices, or the student could make changes on the father, which is the version kept on magnetic tape in a location outside the university offices. Whether the change is made on the son or the father, the two versions will no longer be identical. Therefore, one way to check for changes is to have the computer compare the son with the father.

The university office chooses to do this each time a new father is to be made. After the current transcript versions are ready and before the copy is made on tape, the part of the son that says what the past grades are is compared with what the father, the old copy, says they are. If there is a difference, the system signals a human operator. The person can then look into the matter to see if the computer failed to make a proper match or to see if, in fact, somebody altered the contents of the storage media. When the son and the old version of the father are in proper agreement, a new version of the father is made.

Suppose, however, that a student successfully changes grades on both the son and the father, on both the disk and the tape, so that the two fraudulent transcripts match perfectly. In this case, the computer matching would not detect the fraud. The general truth is that there is a way to get around any security measure. A practical goal is to keep the incidence of computer misuse very low, not to eliminate it completely. Keeping it low means adopting new techniques when deceitful users find too many ways to get around the old security safeguards.

The grandfather system protects against deceit. However, the grandfather system was originally designed to protect against accidental destruction, not intentional distortion, of information. An unskilled computer operator might insert a magnetic disk inside the disk drive in the wrong way and unintentionally destroy thousands of records. A fire, hurricane, or earthquake might devastate the computer records. With backup copies, the father can be obtained and updated using information from the latest source documents, and you are ready to resume operations.

Storing the backup copies in a location some distance from the originals is especially important for protection against natural disasters. Ask your DPers, whether in your own data center or in a service bureau, where the backup copies are stored. There are instances in which the father was kept in a metal cabinet next to the disk drive holding the son. The defense of such a procedure is that a backup copy is easily available in case the original is damaged. This may be true. However, it still would be wise to have an additional copy made and store it at least across the hall, and preferably across town.

There is a relationship between measures taken to protect against intentional distortion and those taken to protect against destruction through human error or natural disaster. The relationship has led to the term "security" being used in a broad sense. A secure system, under this broad definition, is one that performs reliably and provides valid output. There are three closely allied goals in making a system secure. First, there should be little chance any system components will fail to perform in a reliable, valid manner. Next, there should be little impact on other system components if one component fails to perform well. Third, the time to recover from any problem should be minimal.

You will hear "security" being used in this broad sense. Still, there is a good argument that the meaning should be limited to the idea of protecting the computer system against intentional abuse by human beings. The amount of damage that can be done intentionally by people is so great that protection against it deserves a term all its own.

In this sense, security is achieved by minimizing the chance someone can gain unauthorized access to the system, minimizing the damage that can be done if unauthorized access is gained, and minimizing the time to recover from any damage done. It is in this more limited sense that the term "security" is used in this book.

Setting up an environment in which computer security is respected includes employee training. Training, in turn, includes motivation. Employees don't like to do extra work when the work seems needless, and helping to maintain a secure computer system is extra work. Instruct each employee to memorize his or her password and not write it down, since writing down a password is the most common reason it is revealed. But memorizing the password is harder than writing it down. Every employee who uses the computers to manipulate large sums of money should be required to take at least a brief vacation each year. This makes it harder for a thief to cover losses and escape detection. But it also makes it harder for honest, loyal employees to accumulate vacation days.

Certainly keep security measures within reasonable limits. Then use training to motivate employees to enforce those measures. The best motivational stories involve cases in which a breach of security led to employees having to do more work. For instance, tell them about what happened to that organization in Houston. An employee who was angry at the company and expected to be fired placed the following instruction in the system: "Upon issuance of severance pay, erase the customer data base." As soon as the employee was gone, so was the list of records regarding the 1,000 company customers. It cost the company about $50,000 to put together the data base again. However, what motivated those employees to respect computer security is not so much that their employer lost a fair amount of money. It is that, until the data base was rebuilt, the employees were required to do all their record keeping without help from the computers.

Senior managers and major stockholders certainly become concerned when they hear that the organization with which they are associated has lost a large sum of money. Yet, many employees in any organization have ways of assuming the organization will make up a loss and blunder onward as always. When a breach of computer security leads to more daily work for those employees, they quickly become worried.

This is not to say that talk of large sums of money bores the employees. Five hundred thousand dollars, which is not an unusual profit from a computer-assisted embezzlement from a bank, is enough money to get anyone's attention. Even $50,000 is a respectable sum when an employee compares it to his or her monthly salary. Still, if the talk of the large monetary losses goes on for too long, the attention that develops is of the wrong sort. Some employees start thinking, "If old Joe got away with $50,000, why can't I do the same kind of thing?" Because as a society we measure worth primarily in dollars and time, begin computer security training with talk of the large monetary losses for organizations and the quick monetary gains for the computer criminal. Then once you have the attention of the participants, move on to talk about the bother even petty crimes create in the day-to-day workplace.

Stories about quick money gained from computer mischief can inspire workers in the wrong ways. Even worse are case histories describing the specific techniques employed in carrying out the misdeed. There is a company that demonstrated to managers of banks and other financial institutions the ease with which the electronic funds transfer (EFT) network could be tapped and funds diverted to the perpetrator's account. This company sold devices designed to interfere with such system deceit. The demonstration of tapping into the EFT network was part of the sales presentation.

The amount of money transferred over the EFT network during an average week exceeds the value of the annual U.S. Gross National Product, so the sales presentation certainly commanded the attention of the bankers. Also intriguing to the bankers was that the person doing the demonstration described the specific equipment required for the crime, where the equipment could be purchased, and how much it cost, and then showed how to use the equipment. Such information easily increases rather than decreases the amount of EFT fraud.

Successful employee training creates respect for computer security. This environment of respect is so important because of the damage, both short-term and long-term, computer crime does to an organization. There is the direct loss of money. Because of the open trapdoor characteristic of computer crime, these losses can grow as time goes on. Unauthorized disclosure of information from computer files can eat away at company profits and organizational prestige.

The truly insidious effects of security breaches come about because users no longer trust the computer system. This begins with managers deciding they won't put valuable information into the computer system any longer. "Records about my staff don't belong in the company data base from now on," said one manager after the company computers had been victimized. "I'll keep them on paper in files in my office. I can't have some looney tune getting hold of an employee's home telephone number and harassing that employee or using some personal information about an employee to the detriment of my staff member and the company. Being sued for violations of privacy is expensive, especially if we lose the lawsuit. When you straighten out security, come on over and we'll talk. Until then, I'll keep my own information."

It is the most conscientious managers who react like this. Because they usually are the best managers, they'll back down if pushed hard from above. They will put information into the corporate data base. But it will be the most bland information possible or it will be garbage. This then becomes the reputation of the data base. The best employees won't want to put information in, for fear of security leaks, and they won't want to use information from the computer system in making decisions, for fear that the information is overly general or inaccurate.

Unless the organization turns things around and establishes computer security, matters get even worse. The data center loses political power, and precious funds are spent on projects other than keeping computer components up to date. Service bureaus are used less frequently. Decision makers get their information from casual sources and analyze it a piece at a time. The organization fails to use a tool, the computer, that can shave costs, save time, and multiply profits.

Most managers are sharp enough to see such problems developing and to increase computer security. After all, with the importance of automated information processing, the organization might not last long enough to get to the later stages of the scenario. However, many managers again make the mistake of thinking they can't get involved directly because computers involve technical matters. As with the other areas, non-DPers and DPers must collaborate to achieve successful computer security. Don't let the mystique of computers intimidate you.

Don't let DP job titles intimidate you either. One of the larger electronic funds transfer thefts was committed by a man named Stanley Rifkin who had been retained by a West Coast bank as a computer security consultant. Even computer security consultants need to be watched. After completing his consultation, Rifkin returned to the bank, gained unauthorized access using information he'd obtained earlier and, within the workday, made off with over $10.2 million.

Get involved in creating the right environment for computer security. The DPers bring to your collaboration a knowledge of computer system capabilities and flaws. You bring to the collaboration a knowledge of how non-DPers think and act, especially in resisting temptations. The earlier your involvement, the better. Avoid having to be like the executive vice-president who was telling a colleague, "We're looking for an experienced data center manager."

"I thought you just recently hired a data center manager," responded his colleague.

"Yes," said the executive vice-president. "He's the one we're looking for."

Chapter 8

Designs of Success

Decisions about the design of an office have always had an undertone of status. The room used as an office by the Chairman of the Board is not only substantially larger than the room used as an office by the Personnel Manager, the contents of the room are different and are arranged differently, too. Yet when computer equipment comes into any office, functional considerations must go into the mix with the signs of success.

Often the outcome of the mix is amusing. Some of the first middle managers to have terminals in their offices feared their status would suffer because the sight of a keyboard makes one think of clerks, not managers. As a result, much of the furniture for these early innovators had as a primary selling point that the keyboard and screen could be quickly hidden away when not in use. More recently, terminals with small keyboards have become attractive to some executives because it is immediately and abundantly clear to any office visitor that the executive is not using the terminal for routine typing chores. Yet, now that plenty of photographs have appeared in *Business Week* and *Fortune* of top executive officers playing the computer keyboard, managers at all levels are more interested in showing off their terminals than in flipping them into the credenza.

Increased accessibility can lead to increased use. But that's not necessarily so. Organizational funds should be spent on using computers, not just purchasing them as symbols of status. A tenet of office design is to place the equipment where you will use it, and then use it.

Another tenet is "Design for flexibility." Select equipment that you can move easily from one place to another and easily adjust to take account of your individual preferences. Set up your system components so that parts of the configuration can be rearranged without disturbing the entire office. Experiment with the design of your automated office to find what fits you and your co-workers best.

One important reason for selecting adjustable equipment is that people are built differently. Very few individuals are exactly average in how tall they are when seated at a terminal or how long their reach to the keyboard is. The left-handed manager will reject workstations designed for the majority, and the five-foot-tall female executive can feel uncomfortable in the office designed for the former professional wrestler the company recently had to fire.

While you don't want rigidity in the equipment, you do want robustness. The equipment should be strong enough to withstand repeated moves and frequent adjustments. The moves and adjustments occur because the equipment is handed down from one employee to another. Additional computer system components arrive as automation grows in the organization. With the frequent improvements in data processing equipment, these new components are likely to have more sophisticated capabilities. In many organizations, the sophisticated equipment goes to certain departments and the older equipment is handed down to other departments, whose employees have to integrate the equipment into their work styles.

Change occurs for other reasons as well. When the new graphics plotter arrives, the ability to quickly produce hard copy bar graphs and pie charts can dramatically change the sequence of report processing. In turn, this can involve changing the arrangement of the equipment in the office. For the same worker, preferences change, sometimes within the space of one day. A staff member might want the office arranged in one manner while working alone with the computer terminal and in another manner while meeting there with others to review the output from the terminal.

A surprising example of this was provided during a survey completed in one organization of the managers' needs and desires in computer system components. Among the survey tools was a form where the managers were asked to write down their preferences. The response of one manager was as follows:

> "A desk chair with a really quick seat-height adjustment. I want to be able to change the height for meetings with my staff. I have to keep the seat low when working with the VDT and keyboard. I want to keep it high in meetings because that gives authority. My authority is as important as my terminal."

Here was a respondent who hinted that unless he was provided the proper desk chair, he'd be less likely to use his computer terminal. The desk chair was part of the manager's computerized decision making system. More precisely, it was the interaction of the desk chair height, the terminal keyboard height, the terminal screen height, the manager's body dimensions, and his desire for an aura of authority that were part of the computerized decision making system.

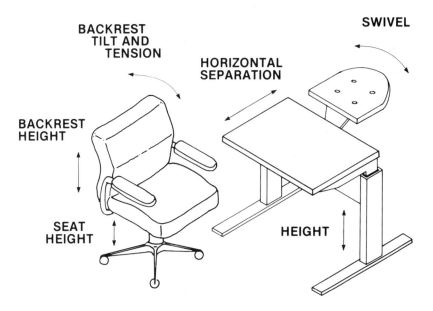

Figure 8.1   Types of adjustability of computer workstation furniture.

Because it was in the interaction, this response also provides a broader meaning to the "Design for flexibility" principle. In the actual situation, this manager's desire was satisfied not by providing a fancier desk chair, but by providing a fancier table for the VDT. The elevation of the keyboard and screen were increased. From then on, that manager could leave the seat where he could maintain a continuous office high. Design offices so that individual needs can be met, with flexibility, from more than one approach.

Figure 8.1 illustrates some of the types of adjustability that are important in office furniture. Height adjustments of the stand and chair help match equipment elevation to the body height of the person using the equipment. There may be some managers in your organization who use terminals while standing up, which could involve a completely different type of VDT stand.

The swivel adjustments help match equipment placement to the body width of the user and allow the screen to be viewed by one person alone at one time and then viewed by a small group at another time. The general theme, again a theme of flexibility, is to design workstations that allow people to work individually and also to work in teams.

If the user has his or her own office, the goal is to have an individual work area that can easily be transformed into a team work area. Figure 8.2 illustrates one of many arrangements that achieve this goal. When the occupant of this office is working alone, he or she faces the desk. The VDT

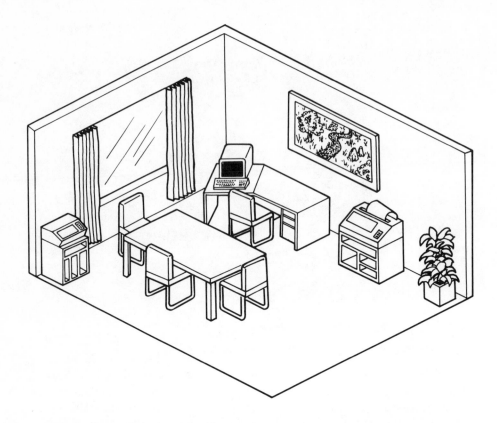

Figure 8.2 Individual automated work area that can be changed into an automated work area for a small group.

and keyboard are directly to the left. A character printer is to the right of the desk, and a graphics plotter to produce charts and graphs is in a third corner of the office. When a small group is to work together in that manager's office, the manager turns the swivel chair around toward the table, and the participants are able to see the image on the VDT screen.

Participants in a meeting want table space. They use it to write notes, to read over printouts, and to simply place books and documents they've taken with them to the meeting. From this standpoint, it is well to place tables between participants. But the consideration from the other side is that members of a small group interact better when there are few physical barriers between them. Especially intimidating to a meeting participant is having the boss's massive desk set between the participant and the boss. The arrangement in Figure 8.2 provides table space, but it does not have the desk placed between participants. Bringing computer components into your office means bringing more potential physical barriers. In Figure 8.2, the equipment is set in places where it won't get in the way during meetings, but the VDT is still in a position where a small group can view the screen together.

Many employees with their own offices don't have the space for a layout like that in Figure 8.2. An alternative is to have meeting rooms set up with VDTs and other computer equipment. There are projectors available that can produce on a meeting room screen the output from a computer system. An advantage of a separate meeting room away from the personal office of any one employee is that each participant is less likely to believe that another participant has a home field edge.

When a few users share a common office area, the goal is to provide for their desire to work individually. Also important is to provide for privacy needs. Computer components seem to bring out in people fears that they are being watched. It is true that managers do frequently use the components to monitor the work performance of subordinates or to raid the data bases of personal rivals. Good security control eases these rational concerns. However, the fears frequently go beyond the rational. For whatever combination of reasons, the fears do exist. Automating a team work area usually increases the desire for privacy within each team member.

Putting up partitions between adjacent work areas is a direct way to provide feelings of privacy. Figure 8.3 illustrates a basic way to do this that can be used in most group work areas. A portable wall about six feet high is placed between adjacent work stations. If there is sufficient space in the room, more partitions can be added.

The difficulty in adding too many partitions is that the users find it harder to work together as a group when they want to. Another, less direct, approach to the problem of privacy takes a more general view of the issue. Privacy has been defined as the control a person is able to exercise over the collection and use of information about himself or herself. The need for privacy is therefore related to the need for control over one's environment, and measures to increase control over a person's environment can ease a person's demands for privacy. In Figure 8.3, the feeling of control for each worker is increased by the individual light fixture at each workstation.

Identifying the human factors like the need for privacy or the desire for a quickly adjustable chair is difficult. Users may not be aware of the factors affecting them. Even if they are aware of the factors, people may hesitate mentioning them because the factors seem to be so subjective. There are many managers who would want a high seat adjustment to feel more authoritative and at the same time would feel foolish writing that down on a survey form. By creating an organizational atmosphere in which experimentation is encouraged, you increase the chances that the human factors in computer use will be dealt with.

Another reason, illogical from a strict engineering view, that people want to change equipment configurations is to personalize the work surroundings. I move into an office previously occupied by somebody else and I inherit all of the person's computer equipment and terminals. Even if the prior occupant

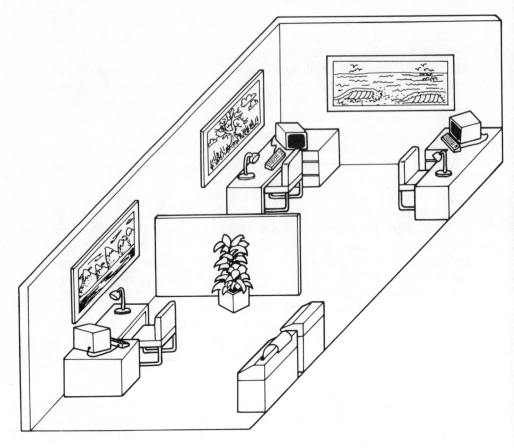

Figure 8.3 Small group work area that provides for privacy needs.

has exactly the same body dimensions I have and precisely the same adjustment preferences, I will still go ahead and rearrange the furniture. It is my way of making the office my own.

This, too, is related to the desire to exhibit control over one's surroundings. Many users are intimidated by a computer, seeing it as superhuman. Many workers hate the cold, heartless efficiency computers represent. Such individuals may show themselves, if no one else, that they are in control by changing the arrangement of the automated office.

A change in office arrangement can come about for other reasons as well. The person might want to stimulate new ways of thinking in the office or may want to signal a new stage in his or her career. These subtle, but crucial, human factors are especially hard to discern because they show up differently in different people. By designing for flexibility, you often solve the problems without needing to diagnose their exact nature.

Some factors in office design are less subtle. Lighting is among them. Good lighting has always been important in the workplace. When that workplace is automated, the nature of the lighting may be different. Glare can be controlled with the proper placement of light fixtures. For example, consider using indirect lighting, in which a light source like a fluorescent tube is placed behind a baffle and the light is then reflected off the ceiling into the work area.

Many kinds of fluorescent lights are hard on the eyes, especially when combined with the chore of reading from a VDT. The light frequencies emitted by those fluorescent lights produce discomfort, and any flicker from the tubes can combine with any flicker from the VDT to cause headaches. It may be best to combine fluorescent with incandescent lighting or with daylight from a window if this can be accomplished while still minimizing glare. In Figure 8.2, notice that the window has drapes. This allows glare from daylight to be controlled. Bright sunshine can be blocked from reflecting off the keyboard. Also notice that the placement of the VDT to the side of the window allows the drapes to be opened without daylight reflecting directly off the screen. For at least part of the day, then, interior lighting can be augmented with natural daylight.

The baffles that help in lighting also help in noise control. Users like moderate, but not extreme, changes in noise levels. The structure of a baffle can absorb sound, and this moderates changes in noise level. The noisiest piece of computer system equipment in the office is almost always the printer. Good printers are acoustically shielded, and many use printing methods so quiet that the loudest sound is the paper spewing through the machine.

Some VDTs emit a high-pitched whine. The source is the device that puts the image on the screen. Because females are, on average, able to hear high frequencies better than males can, women are more likely to be bothered by this sound.

Even-out the general noise level in the office by adding material to absorb sound and covering surfaces that reflect sound. If you need another excuse to get plush drapes for your office, consider the sound they can absorb and their ability to block sound coming through the walls or windows they cover. Since drapes increase sound control much more than carpeting does, you will need to think up other reasons to get the matching plush carpets.

Sound control also can be achieved by actually adding more noise if the noise is of the right kind. Keep in mind that what disturbs users most is not loud noises, but sudden changes in the noise level. The fan from an air conditioner or heater can mask those sudden changes and mask low-level bothersome noises like the VDT's whining. During the periods that the air conditioning and heating are both off, a fan or a device sounding like a fan can be turned on.

Some people say they are calmed and their creativity is enhanced when they hear tape recordings of ocean waves or rainfall. This solution might work best for an individual, since others in the office might be irritated rather than soothed by these associations to a primordial home in the water. Many users say they enjoy a background of conversational sounds in which it is difficult to pick out particular individuals talking. In general, the best masking noises are unobtrusive and even in quality.

The decision maker's choice of noise, as well as the choice of lighting and furniture arrangement, are efforts to humanize and personalize the surroundings. With the same motivation, employees will start decorating the area around computer terminals with flowers and bric-a-brac. Usually this creates no problems for the office equipment since it is not as sensitive to dust as the computer equipment which is located within the data center. However, if this office humanizing extends to drinking coffee where it can easily spill into the keypad workings, there is reason for concern.

In some localities, static electricity is a substantial problem, and those using computer equipment must take care. Computers, in spite of all their astounding processing powers, are paper tigers. An amount of static electricity that would give a person no more than a mild start can destroy computer circuits and jumble the contents of secondary memory devices. You may pass up the plush carpeting not only because you fail to think of a good enough excuse to buy it, but also because walking across the thick carpeting or sliding furniture with casters across it produces static electricity.

Each time a problem like static electricity becomes a bugaboo in office automation, promising solutions appear. Success has been reported with grounded mats that are placed under equipment or on top of carpeting. These mats join other devices coming into the automated office. The devices to project onto a screen in a meeting room an image corresponding to the image on a VDT. Chairs with great stability as well as mobility and with cushioning that adjusts to individual posture characteristics. Sound-absorbing partitions that can be easily moved to accommodate newly arrived equipment.

Design for flexibility to prepare yourself, your co-workers, and your working environment for the rapid changes of office automation. As computer system users become more accustomed to the computers, they will be less intimidated by them. They won't feel so driven to hide the machines inside furniture or behind growing plants or to rearrange the room to assert control. Even then, provide yourself and others the opportunities to make changes. Encourage the attitude of experimentation so important in defusing the potentially destructive subtle human factors. Success for an organization comes when available resources are fully exploited. Within your organization, automated offices designed for flexibility clearly are the signs of success.

Chapter 9

They've Asked For It

Computers coming into a decision maker's life changes things. Strategies, policies, tactics, and procedures are all handled at least a little bit differently. Still, the general rules about using computers in decision making reflect the general rules of all sorts of decision making. This is because the computer is one among many tools used.

A general rule of good management is to talk with the employees. Prepare people for developments by asking them how the developments will affect them. Incorporate employee suggestions into organizational actions. Use employee complaints as an early warning system to spot trouble.

People like to talk and they like to be heard. In demonstrating your willingness to listen, you earn good will even before you take some of the suggestions people give to you. Then consider the suggestions with care. The employees you speak with are often closer to the critical situations than you are. This does mean that their perspective is limited. They may not incorporate into their ideas enough attention to tax considerations, changing market conditions, or reporting requirements of regulatory agencies. The positive side of this limitation is that their focus is sharper. Being closer to the situations, they can detect problems.

All this applies to computerized decision making systems. Talk with those who will be using the components or are using the components and incorporate their suggestions into future plans. The lightning pace of technological developments often means future plans have a short time span. If you learn that a particular component is uniformly bothersome for the decision makers, you can take advantage of that knowledge within a few years, if not a few months, when new components are being selected. A by-product of the rapid technological pace is that most components can be customized to the employee's preferences and still remain compatible with components used by others in the organization. This, too, expands your opportunities to respond when others express their desires.

Human Factors Inventories are tools for assessing those desires. HFIs include interviews and written surveys designed to discover ways to make computer system components more user friendly. Conducting interviews and administering written surveys is a technical skill. In general, it is best if professionals from outside the organization are selected to do the tasks. Many workers, particularly upwardly mobile ones, will talk more freely to an outsider because the workers then have fewer fears of political repercussions. Similarly, if you are evaluating the impressions of a group of employees and you do not need to hook responses to individuals, you will obtain more candor when you grant anonymity to the respondents.

Although it is generally best to use outside consultants for HFIs, the reality is that many organizations conduct such surveys by themselves. Large organizations may have in-house consultants with the technical skills. When these in-house consultants evaluate departments other than their own, they bring many of the advantages of the outsider.

Whether using your own staff or using outsiders, be aware of the important considerations in conducting valid, reliable HFIs. Good timing is toward the top. There are particularly good times to find out from managers what they think of the computer system and what they would like in the components. First, conduct HFIs only when the findings can be used. If a five-year lease has just been signed on a new mainframe, don't ask managers what they want in a new mainframe. It would be useful to ask about concerns they have regarding the new mainframe or what they want in software. However, until mainframe acquisition negotiations are again contemplated, asking managers what they want in a mainframe invites frustration. Respondents do enjoy talking and being listened to. Action-oriented end-users also expect that if they take the time to answer queries with care, their answers will influence the organization's behavior.

Ability to take action is not the same as willingness to take action. In the ideal world, senior managers are forever open to the idea of improvements and surveys are conducted in response to the frequent invitations from senior management. In the actual life of the organization, senior managers are under so many conflicting time pressures that they hesitate inviting new input. Survey findings can be a way to gain the attention of senior management, creating a willingness within their ranks to improve the computer system. This means that it is generally middle managers using the computer system who will initiate the surveys. The HFIs are wedges for making improvements.

The improvements may be intended for current systems, and this brings in another issue of timing. Conduct inventories regarding current systems only after acquainting respondents with the procedures and preparing them for likely changes. Any survey spawns rumors. Combine that with the tendency of automation to arouse suspiciousness in managers, and you conclude that surveys about making computer system users more comfortable can make computer system users less comfortable.

Before conducting interviews or distributing forms, tell the managers why surveys are being carried out and what use is likely to be made of the findings. Perhaps there was a particular event or complaint that signaled the need for a survey. The HFIs might be the initial stage in a feasibility study for new acquisitions, or it might be a routine procedure conducted by rote every two years.

Certainly, your preparation will bias the responses you get. If you tell employees that it is a routine procedure, they'll be less interested in filling out the survey thoughtfully. But the policy of honesty is ultimately best. For the same reasons, don't make promises that can't be kept. If no funds have been allocated for system improvements, the survey should be presented as an inventory of how strong a case can be made to have those funds allocated. Be no more specific than is necessary for honesty, however. Explain that you prefer not to influence answers by saying how you hope the survey comes out. Respondents will speculate, and their perceptions will in fact influence their answers, but don't introduce more bias than is necessary.

If the HFIs are being conducted as part of a major revision of the existing computer system, the proper time for the survey is as soon as possible after news of the general nature of the changes is announced. The survey process helps respondents feel themselves to be part of the changes. This increases their perceptions of control and their consequent support for the new system. The content of the survey responses allows planners to anticipate resistances, thereby providing invaluable data for use in system design.

Computer system revisions are accompanied by anxiety for senior managers and the data processing staff, if not for all the users. You'll detect a pressure to move ahead before survey responses have been carefully analyzed. Certainly, you can't hold out for the purity of controlled research. Yet to the extent possible, caution the prime movers about the dangers in overlooking the human factors. Rushing off in the wrong direction only wastes money faster.

In addition, remember that the computer itself can be used to analyze survey responses. Answers can be coded into categories by interviewers and by those looking over the written forms, and the relative frequencies of answers across categories can be processed by the computer in the same ways that other numerical data are processed.

Sometimes, when a new computer system component is introduced, the old component and new component are operated together for a time. This *parallel operation* provides a backup in the event the new component fails, and it also allows a comparison of the results from the new and old components for quality control. Periods of parallel operation can be excellent opportunities for HFIs. Respondents are able to draw upon comparisons of their experiences with the old and new components as a source of suggestions.

There are cases where the periods of parallel operation are especially busy because employees are taking time to learn how to operate the new component, the new component breaks down, or it is necessary to interact with both components. Even if the employee is not working directly with the situation, he or she might be supervising others who are, and this involves extra time demands. In these cases, respondents will be less cooperative about participating in surveys, and their responses are frequently biased by the stresses they feel. Here, the times right after parallel operation can be better. The stress is less, and the memories are still fresh.

Events external to the changeover can affect timing. For instance, during labor–management negotiations, an opinion survey assumes a different complexion. There are few ideal times to conduct HFIs. Yet, avoid conducting them during periods of great stress on the respondents and at times when potential respondents are likely to feel they are being manipulated by the survey process.

Once the issues of timing are understood, move on to the issue of respondent selection. If you can interview everybody who uses the computer system, that is certainly best. However, when there are hundreds of users, the cost in time and money for complete interviews is prohibitive. Select a representative sample instead. One approach is to type the name of each user on a piece of paper, put the pieces into the biggest hat you can find, and draw out the names of those you'll interview. A better method is to segment the work areas first to be sure you don't completely miss a place where the managers work. If your users are located in six different offices or six different functional departments, be sure that all six are represented among the respondents.

Within each work area to be represented, you might try to select a user who is articulate and aware of the opinions of his or her co-workers. Here, too, there is a better method—random selection. This avoids any appearance of favoritism. If you ask the head of the department or office to select a respondent or two, be careful. The people you get are very likely to be the least skilled. "Let's have Frank go over and talk with them," the head of the department might say. "Frank can't do much useful around here and is always getting in everybody's way. We can only hope it's a nice long interview."

The interview itself should be structured. That is, use a standard set of questions as the basis for the interview. Figure 9.1 is an example of a structured interview. The structure makes it easier for the interviewer, particularly if he or she is inexperienced, since the form tells the interviewer what to say next. The structure also reduces influences from the way the interviewer words a query. At the same time, the interviewer should feel free to explore further themes that come up. Record the wording of additional questions and bring them to the attention of whatever professionals are

Interview Introduction

"As you have heard, the company would like to know what people here think of the computer system. I'll ask you some questions to find out your opinions. To make it easier for me, I'll videotape our interview. I will be looking at the videotape within a few days and using it to add to my notes about our conversation. The General Manager has said that he may look at some of the tapes as well. The tape will be erased one week from today.

"Before I start up the videotape recorder, I want to be sure that is all right with you. May I videotape our interview?"
[If "no"]

"That's fine. If you change your mind while we are talking, please tell me. Or if you would have no objections to my making a sound tape recording with my recorder here, please tell me."
[Leave the sound recorder open to show there is no cassette inside unless it is being used.]

"Next, do you have any questions about the interview?"
[Answer questions briefly. Say that you do not know the answer if that is the case.]

[If it appears to you that the person does not want to participate in the interview:]

"I want you to know that I have been told to cancel interviews with anyone who prefers not to participate. Would you prefer not to be interviewed as part of this survey?"

[If the person asks what steps will be taken, say that you will simply record that fact, but that you have not been told to notify anyone of refusals.]

Interview Questions

1. First, please tell me how you use the computer system in your daily work.
2. What do you think of the company's computer system?
3. In what ways is the system helpful to you?
4. In what ways could the computer system be improved?
5. What complaints do you hear from others about problems with the computer system?
6. What suggestions do you hear, and what suggestions do you have for solving the problems?
7. When you make a mistake on the system, what usually happens?
8. What do you think of those error messages and error routines?
9. How could the error messages and error routines be improved?
10. How about the user manuals? What do you think of them?
11. How could the manuals be improved?
12. What is important to you to have in a computer terminal?
13. How about in the furniture you use?
14. Some people report problems like headaches, eyestrain, backaches, and muscle fatigue when using terminals. Have you had any of these problems? What seems to be the cause?
15. What other suggestions do you have for improving the computer system?
16. Of all the changes or improvements you have suggested, which is, in your opinion, the most important?

Figure 9.1. Example of a Human Factors Inventory

overseeing the survey process. Structure provides guidance, but needless rigidity in the interview is to be avoided.

If you are the interviewer, write notes as the employee answers the questions. This is true even if the interview is being recorded on videotape or audio tape. The tape might be damaged before you can review it. More importantly, by writing down some of what the respondent is saying, you communicate to the respondent that his or her views are being recognized. Then, too, there are respondents who find it hard to talk freely when an interviewer is looking directly at them. In taking notes, you break eye contact while still making it clear to the person that you are listening.

Notice from Figure 9.1 that the interview moves from the general to the specific. This helps respondents open up and provides to the interviewer leads for significant areas to explore. Asking about complaints the manager hears from others is another device to free up the respondent. Some people feel more confident presenting their own views in the context of another person believing it. Mental health professionals at cocktail parties often experience this in hearing stories about, "my next door neighbor," or, "my best friend." Asking about the complaints of others is also simply a way of finding out those complaints. If the person is a good employee, he or she has probably detected significant problems that you would benefit from knowing about.

Another trend in the interview is to move from the negative to the positive. Requests for complaints are followed by requests for suggestions aimed at solving the problems behind the complaints. You don't want to create false hope in the respondent, but you do want to create a genuinely optomistic attitude, and it is best to evaluate your findings in terms of positive actions.

Interview results can be used to construct a written survey. In the survey, open-ended questions are better than multiple-choice questions. The chief advantage of a written survey over interviews is that more people can participate. Appointments don't need to be set up, and the person doing the survey doesn't have to travel from one place to another. The chief disadvantage is that you don't have the opportunity for easy follow-up questions. Your queries must be created with more care.

The wording of questions influences the answers. "What don't you like about the system?" draws a different class of response than, "What do you hate about the system?" Aim for a moderate tone. If a professional is available to review the written survey, even if not to conduct it, use those review services.

No matter how you word questions, you will get an occasional humorous answer. Humor is a fine release of pent-up emotions, and there may be a significant truth behind each joke, but humor does make scoring of responses more difficult. On a written survey, the innocently created question was, "Where do you experience physical discomfort when using the terminal?" One employee, under the cloak of anonymity, responded, "In my office. At my desk." Another, more predictably, wrote a variation of, "It gives me a pain in the behind."

Encourage respondents to type their answers, or at least to print with care, so that the reading of the responses is easier. Some organizations have had successes in asking people to tape-record their answers. In one case, the organization's voice mail system was used in the project. If you select this method, tell the respondents how long the tape will be kept and who will hear it. This will influence the answers you receive, but unless you share this information, most people will assume the tape will be kept forever and anyone can hear it.

Aside from interviews and written surveys, Human Factors Inventories can include observations of the managers at work. You miss a great deal when you ask people what they think of the computers because people are unaware of all aspects of using them or they tell you what they think you want to hear. However, watching people at work consumes a great deal of time and it can produce nervousness in those being observed. You might begin by watching employees use computer output when they participate in meetings. People are less self-conscious being observed in a meeting than being observed individually. In addition, your time as an observer is spent more efficiently, since you'll be watching a number of individuals at once. Then, too, a good proportion of decision making consists of gathering information from others and convincing others, and the meeting is one place where gathering information and convincing others occurs.

Because physical comfort when using computer system hardware is such a crucial human factor, it might seem proper to include measurements of the body dimensions of the managers in HFIs. However, most managers outside experimental laboratories would not find the tapes, gauges, and other aspects of having their bodies measured to be at all proper. Furthermore, it is the need for change over time in the physical arrangement of the components that is the actual crucial factor. Designing for flexibility is more important than designing for an individual user.

Decisions about what to include in HFIs and how to conduct them are made best when you consider how you would react if you were the respondent. In many instances, that is the case. Most of the material above is stated from the perspective of you, or someone you retain, conducting the HFIs on others. In reality, you may be one of the respondents. When you are, you'll likely find that a good way to answer the HFIs is to try out the system components as you go. Accompany interviews and surveys with opportunities to try out the computer system components.

From the perspective of being a respondent, you'll discover that it feels good to participate in HFIs. The content of HFIs assists computer system designers and end-users in selecting and combining components in ways that are most likely to be used by the organization's decision makers. The process of HFIs is also important. When you've a gripe, it's nice to tell somebody about it and it's nice to have your views recognized. The communication process itself eases tension. Then, if the organization takes your suggestion, there is a double bonus. A problem situation has been corrected and your contribution to the organization is enjoyed each time anyone uses the new equipment or procedure.

To maximize these bonuses for the people around you, be sure the summary results of HFIs are distributed to all respondents who request them. During the interview or within the questionnaire, offer to provide results after the series of HFIs has been completed. This motivates people to participate fully. Then, within the summary report, point out how suggestions were used. Sample responses might be given, perhaps identified with the department name of the respondent rather than the person's name, and views aside from the prevailing opinion can be mentioned.

Because of both the content and process advantages, managers derive more value from computer systems in organizations that conduct HFIs. And conducting them is an ongoing process. The issues of timing really reduce to Human Factors Inventories becoming a part of each development in the computerized decision making system, for managers will embrace changes quickly when they see that it was they who requested the changes.

Chapter 10

No More Pigeons

The Parable of the Pigeon

An end-user, with little knowledge of the inner workings of the minds of data processing persons, asks a DPer, "Can pigeons fly?"

"Yes," answers the DPer.

With furrowed brow, the DPer continues. "Unless, of course, the pigeon was just born. Or unless the pigeon is dead.

"Unless you take the dead pigeon, carefully wrap it in tissue paper, place it in a box that you conscientiously seal, and ship that box Federal Express.

"In which case the pigeon can fly.

"If that is what you mean by flying."

The end-user, eyes open wide and teeth clenched tightly, delivers a reminder to the DPer in slow, firm tones. "All I want to know is whether pigeons can fly."

Data processing professionals are conditioned by their job duties to concern themselves with details and with exceptions. The successful among their technical ranks think in bits and bytes, in tiny units of information measurement. Lurking deep within each DPer's brain is the meaning, if not the actual words, from the tale of how the term "bug" came to signify "error" in data processing.

It happened one night during 1945 at Harvard University. A group of data processing pioneers were working on the Mark I, which had been completed a year earlier under financial sponsorship of the International Business

Machine Corporation. Something went wrong that night, and the problem was finally traced to a single circuit within the glass-enclosed computer. Upon further examination, those present saw that a pair of tweezers would be required to remove the problem, for the problem was a lowly moth.

One bug can sabotage an otherwise perfect system. Every single error, every single exception, must command major attention.

Non-DPers are conditioned by their job experiences to think in forests rather than trees. The successful among their ranks avoid being buried under piles of minutiae. When they ask a question, they expect a general answer with the details placed in perspective. Management by exception is attractive only when the range of nonexceptions is broad. Their preferred juxtaposition of potential problems and productive action is expressed in the epigram, "Nothing will be attempted if all possible objections must first be overcome."

These differences between the orientations of the DPer and the end-user create difficulties when the two groups communicate. As an end-user, you see the DPer talking in exceptions, details, and difficulties. Regarding your plan or your equipment, the DPer is telling you why it won't work when you want to know in what ways you can get it to work. On the other side, the DPers see you as talking up there somewhere, at ethereal heights, well above reality.

Clearly, these are pure cases, and exaggerated as well. DPers differ among themselves, as do end-users, and the attitudes of each individual member of one clan or the other depend upon the time and the situation. When a DPer goes to a senior manager to make a case for the purchase of some new million-dollar geegaw, the roles are reversed. The DPer is positively effusive in claiming what the component is capable of, and never mind the details. The non-DPer is cautious, frequently getting enmeshed in the details intentionally to avoid making a decision in a realm where that end-user feels unsure. The arguments of the DPer come across to the non-DPer as unrealistically general, and the responses of the non-DPer impress the DPer as lacking perspective.

This ability to change attitudes is one key to resolving the communication problems. That resolution becomes increasingly important with the growing dependence of organizations upon automation. Skilled end-users know that they must have the help of the computers in order to manage effectively. When they can't get their needs understood, let alone satisfied, by the DPers, the end-users' upset quickly takes on a bitter edge. The DPers are seen as exhibiting tunnel vision. "They focus on computer hardware and software without keeping in mind the overall goals of the organization," the end-users say. "DPers use up money and material and the time of personnel on tasks that are attempted not so much because completion of the tasks supports the organization's mission as because the tasks are technologically challenging."

With this bitter view of DPers as narrow-minded and tactless, end-users start circulating stories like the one about the two programmers who decided to throw caution to the winds and go out to a movie. After sitting through *2001*, in which a computer tries to take over a space mission, they rush out to the lobby to buy refreshments in preparation for *Demon Seed*, in which a computer wants the heroine to bear its offspring.

The DPers' inability to accurately estimate the time span of any project results in them returning after the movie has begun. Popcorn in hand, each carefully makes his way toward their seats. As the first one arrives at the row, he asks the man on the aisle in a concerned tone, "Did I step on your feet on the way out?"

"You most certainly did," whispers the man angrily.

"Carl," the first DPer yells to his partner. "Here's our row."

Friction between end-users and DPers stifles positive creative efforts within the organization. Attention that should be devoted to making better use of the computer system is devoted to struggles for power. Personality conflicts get in the way of collaboration.

Successful resolution of the conflicts begins with realizing that the picture drawn by DPers and end-users of each other are caricatures. The gross exaggeration is good fun only when it encourages people to compromise and change. As an end-user, be tolerant of the detailed responses DPers tend to provide. Respect their expertise and learn from it. What they know can be translated into methods for improving your effectiveness in your organization.

In return, expect DPers to help you in the translation. Listen patiently to the foreign language of computer terminology and then ask how all of this can help you with your daily work. If you don't receive satisfactory answers, persist in your questioning, combining gentleness and firmness.

Develop the ability to get action through informal channels. The DP department in your organization might assign to you a user liaison, and you are told to channel all computer system proposals and complaints through that person. At the same time, you might regularly ride in a car pool with a DPer who is not your assigned user liaison or you might eat lunch with the data center manager. You don't want to sabotage a good working relationship with your user liaison or flagrantly violate the chain of command. Still, if you aren't being provided good service, your car pool and lunchroom contacts may provide some perspective and some answers.

Some frequent themes of misunderstanding between end-users and DPers are the accuracy, timeliness, level of detail, and layout of the data. Regarding accuracy, end-users often have unrealistic expectations of the computer system. In one survey of managers, 70 percent said that before they would accept output from a computer system, they would have to be sure the output was completely accurate. Few managers apply these same standards to information obtained from sources other than the computers. When a manager from one department talks to a manager from another department, each acounts for the fudge factor, realizing the information gathered is rarely 100 percent accurate.

In most situations, you gather information from a variety of sources and compare it to form your impressions. It is hoped that errors in one direction from one source are canceled out by errors in the other direction from another source. You also deal in degrees of confidence and degrees of accuracy. The more information you gather, the more confident you are, and when the information from various sources is in general agreement, you are more confident of the findings. A 90 percent rate of accuracy for the count of the same item in each of 12 warehouses becomes a 95 percent rate of accuracy when the 12 counts are combined because the overestimates tend to balance out the underestimates. If two independent counts agree closely, your faith in the counts increases.

There is a data processing rule of thumb that you pay the same amount of money for the first 75 percent of accuracy, the next 15 percent, and the next 5 percent. This totals up to 95 percent accuracy, and from 95 percent accurate to 99.99 percent accurate, the costs escalate wildly. Conscientious DPers do their best to provide you 100 percent accuracy if that is what you insist upon. However, the costs can be prohibitive.

Accuracy is more important in some circumstances than in others. Calculating the trajectory of an airborne missile with extreme accuracy holds priority over calculating amounts of available inventory with that same degree of accuracy, both because of the effects of inaccuracy and because of the time allowed for adjustment whenever inaccuracies are discovered.

Timeliness is a second area in which misunderstandings frequently occur between DPers and end-users. "How quickly do you need your output?" asks the DPer. The manager's knee jerk response is, "Immediately." But what you mean by immediately might differ from what the DPer means. Is a predictable wait of 40 seconds immediate? For you that might be soon enough, where the DPer might think you are asking for a response time of less than one second.

As with issues of accuracy, your needs for a timely response depend upon the situation. Actually, there are two issues. First, how far in advance can you anticipate that you will be making a request? Second, once you have made the request, how quickly must you have the response from the computer system? As an example, you might want a computer analysis of sales figures for an upcoming meeting. You want the very latest figures, so you'd like to be able to make your request as close as possible to the meeting time. In this sense, you want a quick response. Along with this, you know when the meeting is scheduled, so time can be reserved on the computer system in advance. In this sense, your lead time requirements are not severe.

Remember that an unpredictable response time is often more bothersome than a long response time. Also remember the troubles created for computer systems by the natural ambiguities of non-DP managers' language. When talking about the timeliness of a response, define your terms. If you are asking a question of the data base, response time for you is probably the interval from when you enter your request until the answer appears on the VDT screen. However, if you need hard copy, the response time for you probably includes the wait until the printer is done. If you are doing data entry, your definition of response time is likely to be the interval from when you enter one item of data until the system indicates it is ready to accept the next item of data.

Level of detail is the third theme of misunderstandings. You may want the monthly summary figures, but you are getting the daily figures. At the same time, you may have spotted a source of trouble in a specific program and you want the most detailed figures possible so that you can discover the source of the problem. When flexibility has been the prime criterion in computer system design, especially data base design, end-users will have an easier time obtaining the desired level of detail. Still, there will always be ad hoc requests that the system can't quickly satisfy. To the degree possible, let DPers know in advance what you require and try to estimate the costs.

Because many DPers work on tasks that take months or years to complete, they often are accustomed to job specifications that change slowly. These staff can experience trouble in understanding why your requirements change so frequently. Such an understanding involves an appreciation of the unpredictability in the end-user's duties.

Layout of the information on the printed page or on the terminal screen is another theme of misunderstandings. The manager's brain incorporates information better when the information is formatted in certain ways. For example, as a general rule, the manager's eye moves from left to right and from top to bottom when reviewing information. When comparing numbers, the manager prefers those numbers to be side by side, as in Figure 10.1A, instead of one directly above the other.

Lacking any further information from the end-users, the DPer would then do well to employ these general guidelines in designing the physical arrangement of the output. Hopefully, though, the DPer will discuss preferences with the end-users, and the preferences sometimes differ from the general rule. In skimming information, rather than reading it, for instance, the manager's eye usually starts at the upper left, moves in a spiral for a brief time, and then settles into the left-to-right, top-to-bottom pattern. Some managers might want certain types of data arranged like those in Figure 10.1B, with the numbers to be compared vertically adjacent instead of horizontally adjacent.

Report generators, a type of software, allow you, as a non-DPer to decide how you want your output to be formatted and to put those instructions directly into the computer system. You save time for yourself and for the DPers when you carry out this chore yourself. The format is also more likely to be what you desire because you can change the format when it no longer

Company	Sales ($ million)		Profits ($ million)	
	This Year	Last Year	This Year	Last Year
Amer Indus	134.9	140.4	−4.6	−4.9
Bench Corp	145.5	123.3	0.8	6.7
Comm Manuf	56.7	55.6	2.3	1.8
Daily Prod	214.3	133.1	23.5	13.6
Excel Tool	182.5	164.4	15.4	13.8
Futur Labs	35.8	37.2	2.0	3.2

A. Numbers to be compared are side by side

Company	Amer Indus	Bench Corp	Comm Manuf	Daily Prod	Excel Tool	Futur Labs
Sales *($ million)*						
This Year	134.9	145.5	56.7	214.3	182.5	35.8
Last Year	140.4	123.3	55.6	133.1	164.4	37.2
Profits *($ million)*						
This year	−4.6	0.8	2.3	23.5	15.4	2.0
Last Year	−4.9	6.7	1.8	13.6	13.8	3.2

B. Numbers to be compared are vertically adjacent

Figure 10.1. Two formats for presentation of data

meets your needs and because there is one less link where matters can get lost in translation. Rather than communicate your needs to the DPers, who then communicate them to the computer system, you communicate your needs to the computer system yourself.

In other ways as well, non-DPers are able to develop specificiations for computer systems without requiring the assistance of DPers. Still, the DP staff members are excellent resources for learning about the computer system features that allow more direct communication. There are also many circumstances where the DPers' help and intervention is, in fact, necessary.

Good communications between DPers and end-users is an ongoing process. Follow up and follow through. There are too many instances in which an end-user and DPer meet, the end-user describes requirements to the DPer, the two go off their separate ways, and the two meet again only after the DPer views the task as finished. It should be no surprise when the completed work of the DPer has only a passing resemblance to the current requirements of the end-user. Because the two did not confer during work on the project, the DPer has had no opportunity to correct for misunderstandings of the end-user's wishes and for changes over time in the end-user's specifications.

Many data processing departments now use concepts of *modular programming*, in which software is created as a system of interrelated packages, called modules. Until each module is developed in full, a "dummy module" is used in its place. The advantage to you is that you can try out a program or portions of a program while they are being developed. It is something like meeting with an interior decorator to develop a plan for your new home and then visiting the house while it is being decorated so that you can discuss desired changes with the professional. The dummy modules are like full-size cardboard replicas of your undelivered furniture that allow you to judge how things will be when the specifications have been fulfilled.

Tools like report generators and modular programming allow you to become more personally involved in meeting your own specifications. A step beyond that is for you to increase your data processing expertise, and a logical extension of that is for you to become a DPer yourself. One result of the burgeoning user friendliness of data processing is that people without substantial engineering experience can readily learn to function well in some DP jobs. Certainly, special interests and aptitudes are required, but they are interests and aptitudes found outside a data center as well as within it. Employees from Accounting or Manufacturing can possess the talents for success in the Data Processing Department or, as it is becoming known in many organizations, the Information Resources Department. What better way to improve communications with DPers than to have former end-users in some of those positions. User-friendly DP makes it easier to hire DPers from outside the traditional DP ranks, and DPers hired from outside the traditional DP ranks are especially likely to make DP more user friendly.

Whatever it takes to accomplish it, collaboration between you and DPers is necessary if your organization's computer systems are to help all of you achieve full potential. Collaboration involves frequent discussions, both scheduled and unscheduled, among the various groups able to make use of the computers. Along with producing better system specifications that can be corrected during system development, collaboration builds an atmosphere of trust. Trust, in turn, allows the users to work together as a true team, dividing duties and delegating responsibilities.

The virtues of collaboration, communication, trust, teamwork, division of responsibilities, and delegation. Things are much the same as before the computers came in the door. These powerful tools change the specific methods your organization employs in decision making. However, when used properly, computer systems leave intact the best approaches toward making decisions.

Index